The American Balfou

CW00922943

THE ORIGINS OF U.S. SUPPORT FOR ZIONISM 1917-1922

by

Paul Azous

Acaday Press

The American Balfour Declaration

The Origins Of U.S. Support For Zionism

1917-1922

Text Copyright © 2013 Paul Azous
ISBN 978-1-936778-62-1

Author Website: www.paulazous.com

Author Email: info@paulazous.com

Published by:
Acaday Press
P.O. Box 10474
Jacksonville, FL 32247 USA

1-904-638-5397
www.acaday.com

All rights reserved.

No part of this publication may be copied, translated, reproduced, stored in a retrieval system, or transmitted in any form or by any means, electronic, mechanical, photocopying, recording or otherwise, without prior permission in writing from the publisher.

For my wife Tamar,
of whom the blessing is most fitting

... אשר ברא ששון ושמחה, חתן וכלה, גילה רינה, דיצה וחדווה, אהבה
ואחווה, ושלום ורעות ...

... who created joy and gladness, groom and bride, mirth,
song, delight and rejoicing, love and harmony and peace and
companionship ...

Contents

Zionism: *A movement that began in the late 19th Century, aiming to create a Jewish national home in the ancient homeland of the Jews, the land of Israel.*

◆ ◆ ◆

Zionism denotes both the age-old longing of the Jews for the return to Zion, or Jerusalem, and the land of Israel and the "ism", the goal to create a modern nation-state.

Thus, Zionism was a movement seeking to return the Jews to their ancient homeland utilizing modern political nationalism.

Following the creation of the State of Israel in 1948, Zionism's main goals were nurturing the new state and bringing Jews from far corners of the world to it.

Introduction

His Majesty's Government view with favour the establishment in Palestine of a national home for the Jewish people, and will use their best endeavours to facilitate the achievement of this object, it being clearly understood that nothing shall be done which may prejudice the civil and religious rights of existing non-Jewish communities in Palestine or the rights and political status enjoyed by Jews in any other country.

Balfour Declaration
(November 2, 1917)

Be it resolved by the United States Senate and House of Representatives, that the United States of America favors the establishment in Palestine of the national homeland for the Jewish people, in accordance with the provisions contained in the Declaration of the British Government of November 2, 1917, known as the Balfour Declaration, it being clearly understood that nothing shall be done which may prejudice the civil and religious rights of non-Jewish communities in Palestine, or the rights and political status enjoyed by Jews in any other country, and that the holy places and religious buildings and sites in Palestine shall be adequately protected.

Palestine Lodge-Fish
Resolution (September 1922)[1]

After the proclamation of the landmark Balfour Declaration of November 1917, many supporters of Zionism hoped that the American government would announce its support of the Zionist undertaking: the establishment of a Jewish national home in Palestine, the ancient homeland of the Jews.

Official American affirmation of the Balfour Declaration, they thought, would quash nearly all Britain's apprehension regarding Zionism, and the gates of Palestine would swing open for the Jews sooner rather than later. Indeed, following the split and almost utter collapse of the Zionist movement at the Cleveland Conference of June 1921, Chaim Weizmann, the movement's leader, expressed his belief that America's support was necessary to re-strengthen Zionism. Additionally, US support for the Balfour Declaration, he asserted, would be a quintessential step towards achieving Zionism's goal of statehood. Indeed, from 1917-1922 the American people (and by extension the American government) had become increasingly more supportive of the Zionist movement, eventually managing to garner endorsement for a pro-Zionist proclamation from both houses of Congress and the president: the "Palestine Lodge-Fish Resolution" of 1922.

Many historians and laymen have been led to believe, inaccurately, that America's involvement with Zionism began with the Truman administration after the end of World War II. In fact, it was twenty-five years earlier when the entire American government went on record for the first time in favor of creating a Jewish national home in Palestine, in the Lodge-Fish Resolution. This book details a crucial, unknown history of American Zionism in the first quarter of the 20th century and demonstrates how it paved the way for Truman's crucial support for the creation of the modern state of Israel in 1948. Until now, this period – and in particular this episode – has been almost entirely absent from historical scholarship.

The proclamation of the Palestine Lodge-Fish Resolution and the events leading up to it, in particular, has been neglected by both American Jewish historical scholarship and Zionist history for nearly a century. Only brief excerpts from the resolution and a few references to it have been discussed in various academic works. None of these provides a complete picture of the historic Congressional bill, nor do they reveal what prodded President Warren G. Harding to sign it – or why several years transpired before the resolution finally was brought to the Congress for a vote.

In this book we will see how the five years between the passing of the Balfour Declaration in 1917 and the Palestine Lodge-Fish Resolution in 1922 brought several striking changes to America itself, and how these changes ultimately led to the passage of America's first official pro-Zionist proclamation.

Three Elemental Changes

What developments in American life helped shift the US government towards supporting the Zionist movement?

1) By the end of World War I, *social changes* in the United States led many ordinary American citizens to support the creation of a national Jewish home in Palestine, due largely to the practical needs of the Jews the world over. Massive persecution and displacement during WWI – and of course, even before that – had helped convince many Americans that the creation of a Jewish home would actually save lives. Cognizant of the persecution of European Jewry, Americans were sympathetic; they did not expect the American government to turn a blind eye to such maltreatment.

2) *Religious change* among Christians, as well as greater tolerance and acceptance, also played a role in America's support of a Jewish national home in Palestine. This is not to say that the majority of Protestant Americans were philo-Semites; however, they did differ significantly from their Catholic counterparts in their biblical exegesis on the Jews, the land of Israel and the second coming of Christ. For centuries, Catholicism had asserted that the Jews were branded with the mark of Cain, destined to wander the earth for eternity for the rejection of Jesus. Protestant teachings were less extreme, which helped mainstream Protestants increasingly perceive Jews as a people with rights rather than the anti-Semitic stereotypes that had prevailed for centuries. Protestant theology's coming to terms with the Jews and their place in Christian thought impacted many of the Protestant sects in the US.

3) The social changes and religious sentiments of American citizens led directly to the third new element in America: *political support* of Zionism after the World War I, a result of the persecution of European Jews, the ensuing refugee situation in Europe, and Christian messianic beliefs. Many politicians, including the president of the United States, had called for the creation of a Jewish national home in Palestine. Although Zionism had its antagonists in every sector of the US government, there was a stronger voice of support. Politicians supported an explicit US affirmation for Zionism for a number of reasons, among them religious ideals, the wish to see historic justice done for a persecuted people, and the belief that a Jewish national home in Palestine would be an eventual ally of the United States. Additionally, with Great Britain in control of Palestine and backing the endeavor, many US officials maintained that a resolution – constitutionally weaker than a law – was not so strong that it would entangle the US in any foreign affair. Until the Palestine Lodge-Fish Resolution, though, there was no official government support for the creation of a Jewish homeland in Palestine. This is where the "alliance of four" came to play a pivotal role.

The Alliance of Four

The success of the resolution in 1922 resulted, I argue, from an odd alliance between a member of the House of Representatives, two Senators, and an immigrant Orthodox Rabbi. These four parties came together in order to lobby and push for the passing of a pro-Zionist resolution. Senator Henry Cabot Lodge, the staunch "selective" isolationist from a Blueblood Boston family, came out in full support behind Rabbi Simon Glazer, the chief architect of the Zionist lobbying campaign from the years 1921-1922. Lodge, arguably one of the more powerful Senators in US history, sponsored the resolution in the Senate and gave nudges to those who opposed or were tepid to the Zionist movement. Congressman Hamilton Fish of New York actively supported Zionism and was the sponsor of the resolution in the House of Representatives. Senator Charles Curtis, the first Native American elected to the Senate, used his influence to have Rabbi Glazer meet various politicians, and opened the door for Glazer to eventually meet with the President of the United States. Rabbi Glazer, an unlikely figure who was not one of the leaders of the American Zionist movement, almost singlehandedly led the Zionist campaign to convince the American government – from top to bottom – that the creation of a Jewish national home was mandatory to support. This book tells the story of how these four figures and their odd alliance were able to move the American Congress and President to throw their weight behind the emerging Zionist movement through an official American endorsement of Zionist aims.

The Palestine Lodge-Fish Resolution put the US government squarely in the Zionist camp. Thus, the Resolution is, to some standard, the single most important legislative piece in American Zionist history. This work will focus on the process that produced the Palestine Lodge-Fish Resolution and touch upon the impact of America's "Balfour Declaration". It will be argued that the Palestine Lodge-Fish Resolution appears to be the most significant political achievement of the Zionist movement since the passage of the actual Balfour Declaration five years prior, and indeed it is the most significant document in American Zionist history until 1948.

Sources and My Contribution

Most of the information utilized for this book was taken from primary sources, including material from Congressional records, the

American Jewish archives, American Zionist archives, Presidential libraries and writings, Zionist memoirs, as well as various newspapers, synagogue clippings, and telegrams. A full list of all sources can be found in the bibliography of this work.

For nearly 90 years historians that mention the Palestine Lodge-Fish Resolution in their historical works either devote one or two lines referencing that the Congress and President supported such a resolution – no history is given of this undertaking – and those that wrote even more than this attribute the success of the passing, not to its rightful architect, but inadvertently to others.

Nearly every earlier historian who touched upon this topic credited the success of the Resolution to the efforts of Justice Louis Brandeis, American Jewry's leading Zionist advocate at the time. My own research, however, indicates that although he played an important role in the Zionist movement he was a relatively marginal figure in the Lodge-Fish Resolution's passage. In all sources that I have analyzed, including primary material that was unavailable to earlier historians, Brandeis is simply not mentioned in any dealings in the Senate, the House of Representatives or the Executive Branch. The pivotal player in the unfolding events of the Palestine Lodge-Fish Resolution was a rabbi named Simon Glazer, who is glaringly absent from previous historical research. This work will hopefully shed new information regarding the major players and historical events in this unfolding process.

Although many have written about the history of Zionism in America, I believe that all such works lack the entire picture, as nearly all mainstream works do not even mention this first American resolution supporting the creation of a Jewish national home, let alone details its history. I hope that this book, which has been developed and researched as part of my PhD dissertation, will help rewrite a portion of American Zionism that for almost a century has been neglected by history.

Even though the Palestine Lodge-Fish Resolution was forgotten by history, it is still important because it set the wheels in motion for the important relationship between the United States and Zionism. The Resolution paved the way for Zionism to become part of the discourse of American politics, inside both Houses of Congress and inside the Executive branch, even until this very day.

Christian Zionism In America

Many Americans had supported the return of the Jews to their ancient homeland for decades before the Palestine Lodge-Fish Resolution officially endorsed the idea in 1922. Although Zionist groups had been lobbying for several years to secure the US government's support for their goal, their efforts were intensified only after the San Remo Conference in 1920, convened to ratify and implement the recommendations made by the Allied Supreme Council at the Paris Peace Conference the previous year.[2] In the United States, large swathes of citizens – devout Christians in particular – were enthralled with the idea of restoring the Jews to the Promised Land, largely because of their messianic hopes but also because of Jewish refugee issues that surfaced after World War I.

Once Zionism obtained the backing of the US government, there was a palpable transition in the approach of these American enthusiasts: "sympathetic Zionism" (sympathy for the plight of suffering Jews, who obviously needed a home of their own) gave way to "tangible Zionism" (political support for a people with national rights).[3] Tangible Zionism garnered a large number of advocates, among them lay, religious and civic leaders.

The aspiration of many Americans for a Jewish return to Palestine is in fact as old as the United States itself.[4] The country's founding fathers, including George Washington, Thomas Jefferson and Benjamin Franklin, related to their new nation in terms of "Manifest Destiny," maintaining that through divine intervention, God had created the United States as the new "Promised Land," and its people the "New Israel." So fervently did they believe that America was chosen personally by God that, in the aftermath of the Revolutionary War of 1776, a debate raged between the new nation's ideological and political figures: What symbol should represent the United States on the country's national seal? After several biblical ideas were rejected, e.g. the epic splitting of the sea, the eagle was chosen. What is significant about this tale is that John Adams, later the second president of the United States, was one of the first to express support publicly for a renewed Jewish nation. He wrote, "I really wish the Jews again in Judea an independent nation for, as I believe, the most enlightened men of it have participated in the amelioration of the philosophy of the age."[5] Hence there is a clear correlation between early colonial and presidential support for the idea of restoring the Jews to the land of Israel.[6] From the nation's earliest days, both Christian religious belief and sympathy for an oppressed people underlay America's espousal of Zionism, but the more compelling explanation, as least until the first quarter of the 20th Century, was certainly messianic Christianity. We will see in a later chapter how some American presidents saw themselves as no less than the catalyst for the world's redemption – an evangelical concept based on the precondition that the Jews must all be returned to their homeland before the second coming of Christ – and how some Jews played on these Christian aspirations.

Although not a statement of policy, John Adams' sentiments resonated well into the present era, when Christian theology met up with political reality, and the concept of meting out historic justice for the Jews found a practical means to realize its goal.[7] Adams' statement, and similar ones throughout the following century, had no political repercussions. Later presidents were also said to endorse the return of the Jews to Palestine, but no practical measures were undertaken towards that goal. Immediately after his Emancipation Proclamation of January 1, 1863, for instance, Abraham Lincoln met with a Christian Zionist named Henry Wentworth Monk, who expressed his keen desire that the Jews return to the Promised Land and rebuild their country. Apparently his motivation was religious, spurred by the persecution of the Jews in Russia and the Ottoman Empire as anti-Semitism mounted in both places. Lincoln was said to have replied to Monk that the return of the Jews to the Holy Land was "a noble dream and one shared by many Americans."[8] Lincoln's statement, of course, long preceded the creation of the political Zionist movement, but his message echoed previous and subsequent presidents: The Jews should one day return to their land. The sentiments of men like Adams and Lincoln stemmed from their upbringing as believing Christians as well as from their political awareness: a Jewish national home was needed to alleviate Jewish persecution. Nevertheless, it would be many years until any practical measures were taken to expedite the creation of Jewish homeland.

It appears that the Christian dream of returning the Jews to their homeland took on new urgency after deadly pogroms in Russia throughout the 1880s and particularly in 1891, which claimed many Jewish victims, and forced thousands more to flee. Such Russian pogroms underscored the need to solve the issue of Jewish persecution. They had been unleashed not by some fringe elements of society but under the direct auspices of Czar Alexander III, the ruler of Russia. When his father, Czar Alexander II, was assassinated in 1881, the Jews were quickly (and wrongfully) blamed, leading to a decade-long outburst of virulent attacks culminating in 1891, when anti-Semitic rioting throughout the country was accompanied by the expulsion of some 20,000 Jews from Moscow.

For the most part, however, the ensuing refugee problems were not new. Thousands of Jews had already made their way out of Russia, either because of physical, social, political or economic coercion, beginning in 1881. Many of those refugees ended up penniless and as far away as Istanbul. American and British diplomats stationed there in the 1880s, namely General Lewis Wallace and former British M.P. Lawrence Oliphant, testified that some Jews were starving to death in the streets.[9] This led many believing Christian Americans to the conclusion that anti-Semitism would be eliminated if the Jews had a home of their own.

In response to the atrocities in Russia, several hundred prominent Christian Americans signed what came to be known as the Blackstone Memorial (dated March 5, 1891), a petition for the creation a Jewish homeland created by William E. Blackstone, a wealthy and prominent Evangelical Methodist leader. Blackstone wanted the Jews restored to their homeland primarily to fulfill the prophetic Christian prerequisite for Christ's second coming, but also to alleviate Jewish suffering. His petition, which he sent to President Benjamin Harrison and his Secretary of State, James Blaine, for approval, stated that the United States should call an international conference with the intent that the world

> ...should consider the condition of the Israelites and their claims to Palestine as their ancient home, and to promote, in all other just and proper ways, the alleviation of their suffering condition.[10]

Political inferences helped support Blackstone's thesis. In some respect, his rationale resembled that of European powers who, particularly after World War I, were literally, and in many cases arrogantly, deciding how to divide up the world – including Africa and the Middle East – they had just conquered. Blackstone remarked:

> Why not give Palestine back to them [the Jews] again?

According to God's distribution of nations it is their home –
an inalienable possession from which they were expelled by
force...Why shall not the powers which under the treaty of
Berlin, in 1878, gave Bulgaria to the Bulgarians and Servia to
the Servians now give Palestine back to the Jews...If they could
have autonomy in government, the Jews of the world would rally
to transport and establish their suffering brethren in the time-
honored habitation...Let us now restore to them the land of which
they were so cruelly despoiled by our Roman ancestors."[11]

Blackstone aimed to obtain endorsement of the petition by the
president of the United States, who would then presumably gather the
support of other international leaders to bring about a Jewish homeland.[12]
It was ultimately signed by some of America's most prominent citizens,
among them the Chief Justice of the Supreme Court; the Speaker of
the House of Representatives (and later President) William McKinley;
John D. Rockefeller, and many others.[13]

Numerous signatories were motivated by evangelical sentiments,
as it was believed that the return of the Jews to the Holy Land would
spur the beginning of the Christian redemption.[14] It is also intriguing
that many of the signatories of the petition, including McKinley –
although somewhat resonating a conspiracy tone – were affiliated with
the Freemasons and the Knights Templar, the secretive brotherhood
whom many claim attempt to control the world through political and
economic means. It is likely that McKinley saw in this first influential
"Zionist" political process that, by returning the Jews to Israel, he
would be fulfilling one of his Masonic duties.[15] President Harrison,
however sympathetic to the plight of the Jews as well as sensitive of the
influential power of the signatories, rejected the Blackstone Petition.[16]

It would not be until several years later, in 1897, that the first Zionist
Congress convened in Basel, Switzerland, where a political body of
Jews gathered to plan and orchestrate an eventual creation of a Jewish
national home in Palestine. Led by Theodor Herzl, an assimilated Jew
who was looked on as the leader of the growing movement, Zionism
was about to get an infusion of both political will and needed capital.
As a political movement, Zionism appeared to gain more popularity
throughout Europe and the West, prompting the expansion of Christian
groups in the Middle East.

For instance, during this time, American missionaries were busy
attempting to spread their message throughout Palestine and beyond.

Although for the most part missionaries did not have an organized lobby, many political figures came to recognize their need. As opposed to the European colonists of the Middle East and elsewhere, American missionaries posed little physical threat to foreign peoples, as they rarely exploited commercial happenings and posed no danger militarily. Many also taught locals to read and write. In response, local inhabitants ranging socially from the ruling family to the common village dweller gave their trust and appreciation.[17] However, even though thousands of missionaries traveled to such regions as Syria, Lebanon, and Egypt, and unlike other places such as the sub-Indian continent, they were highly unsuccessful in their endeavors to convert Jews or Muslims.[18] These missionaries paved the way for later American development in the region, and in particular in Palestine, for through their contacts with local politicians and businessmen, much bureaucracy could be avoided for American enterprises.

Simultaneous to the missionaries came the "Adventist Colonies," Christian communities set up in the Holy Land for the specific purpose of waiting for the imminent return of Jesus to the world.[19] Many Americans found a warm place to stay at these centers, whether they were businessmen, pilgrims, or archeologists, and this helped to encourage US involvement in the region, particularly tourism. More and more, and particularly since the creation of Israel (yet even a century before its founding) these Adventist Colonies and those from the evangelical camp supported Zionism for ulterior motives. Their main reason for supporting the creation of a Jewish state was an interpretative Christian prerequisite for the second coming of Jesus, that being the so called "rapture." In this pre-Armageddon (*Gog U-Magog*) scenario, all Christians are literally brought up to heaven prior to God judging the world and most likely destroying it. Of all the Jews, 144,000 are said to bow down to Jesus, the true messiah, and be saved, while the rest of the millions will literally be wiped out in the greatest holocaust ever.[20] The 144,000 remaining Jews will be left alive in order to testify that Jesus is the true messiah. Hence, there is a need for the Jews to be in the land of Israel – and most likely must have the Third Temple in use – for the rapture to transpire.[21]

Regardless of how many late 19th Century prominent Americans believed in the rapture or not, an underlying current was that many supported the return of the Jews to the land of Israel. Coupled with the feelings of religious fervor and the political happenstance of the Jews, justice, in more than one way, would be served if the Jews had a home of their own. As the years passed, it became more common for political and religious groups to support the creation of a Jewish state, so that by the end of World War I, when both political sentiments and Christian emotions were running high for such a cause, the concept and practicality for a Jewish state became more real. This idea was grounded on two main assumptions: That a strong and dominant pro-American presence in the Middle East, as will be illustrated, is strategically good foreign policy, and that a Jewish state would be an ally of such a platform; and that the Christian eschatological philosophy of the End of Days, that lingered in the hearts and minds of Christian America, would soon come about.

This Christian messianic vision, which had been theoretical for centuries took on new meaning and practicality with General Allenby's "conquest" of Jerusalem in 1917 and then with the issuance of the Balfour Declaration shortly after. With Jerusalem and the Holy Land under Christian control for the first time in nearly a thousand years, and the Jews about to re-enter world affairs by acquiring the Holy Land once again, Christian messianic aspirations ran high.[22] These sentiments permeated many members of Congress and the Executive Branch, which more than likely played a significant role in many supporting a pro-Zionist position.

Significantly as well, and more pertinent to the pro-Zionist congressional debates of 1922, leaders in the Congress asserted that both American and Christian ideals were alive and well, so much so that not to lend support to the creation of a Jewish national home would be betraying their Christian teachings. Congressman Theodore Frank Appleby of New Jersey, who wanted his own language included in the future resolution, wrote that

> One of the greatest sources of pride of an American-born citizen is to hold aloft the land of his birth. The oft-repeated refrain of the poet –
>
> Breathes there a man with soul so dead, Who ne'er unto himself has said, This is my own, my native land?
>
> – Is but an outburst from one of the deepest wells of the human heart. And for the Jewish race, which gave Christianity to the world and brought to civilization its highest and noblest inspiration, a race which embraces some of our greatest bankers,

merchants, lawyers, educators, and leaders in every line of the world's activities to be no longer denied a country which they can call their own is a humiliation too deep for the pride of an American.

Fellow members, the resolution before you embodies the faith of the Jewish people and gives expression to its longing which has never forsaken them. It should be the privilege of the House of Representatives to pass this resolution. It should be the privilege of any Christian nation to help make the cradle of Christianity again the center of civilization instead of permitting it to devastation and epidemics, which it has now been for centuries.[23]

Leaving the religious undertones aside, from the beginning of the 20th Century through the creation of the State of Israel in 1948, Zionism had many battles to wage, including convincing the Jews that it was a right cause to support. Yet as the political climate changed in the first quarter of the century, particularly on the ground in Palestine by the *Yishuv's* growth (the Jewish community in Palestine) as well as the British occupation of the land, so too would the Zionist movement move forward. Once the Balfour Declaration was issued in 1917, the Zionist movement became closer to its goal. Nevertheless, the nearer the prospects of a state came, the more obstacles were placed in the path of its birth. Many of these obstacles, it was felt in the Zionist movement, could be relegated to minor impediments if the United States gave its endorsement of the Balfour Declaration.

The Immediate Influence Of The Balfour Declaration In America

The Balfour Declaration of November 2, 1917 greatly influenced Congressional representatives in the United States, paving the way for the American government to support the creation of a Jewish homeland in Palestine. The Balfour Declaration of November 2, 1917 states the following:

> His Majesty's Government view with favor the establishment in Palestine of a national home for the Jewish people, and will use their best endeavors to facilitate the achievement of this object, it being clearly understood that nothing shall be done which may prejudice the civil and religious rights of existing non-Jewish communities in Palestine or the rights and political status enjoyed by Jews in any other country.[24]

After centuries of being stateless the Jews were finally to have a home again of their own. It was a triumphant time for the Zionist movement. Yet reactions to the Balfour Declaration were varied, particularly among world Jewry, who for the most part, was not united on the Zionist cause. Numerous nation-states and most of the Islamic world also opposed any change in the status quo of Palestine, most notably the Arabs, the Vatican and other Catholic enclaves such as France and Brazil. Public opinion too varied, particularly within the Jewish community of England where a heated debate between Jewish nationalism on the one hand, and loyalty to her Majesty's Government on the other, engulfed British Jewry. In the United States, reactions were also mixed. It would only be months later after Balfour that the Zionist movement, infused with new life by the declaration, would turn its attention to America in the battle for support. For many Zionists asserted, in particular Chaim Weizmann, the head of the movement, that with American support, "the doors of Palestine would be opened and every objection on the part of every nation would be removed;" thus the Jews would be one step closer to acquiring an independent Jewish state.[25]

As noted from the previous chapter on Christian Zionism, messianic expectations and the belief in the second coming of Christ were central beliefs of many Americans, particularly in the 19th Century. Once the Balfour Declaration was issued a new frenzy was initiated among Christian groups in the United States and England. This included the creation of prayer groups, the drafting of spiritual pamphlets and books, and eventual fund raising, both for Jewish settlement and for conversion purposes. With politics now in play, many American Christians found a new avenue to support or expedite the second coming of Christ. With the Jews and their projected state at a visible position in world politics, America, for the most part, supported the Zionist endeavor.

Politically, though, even before Balfour's 1917 proclamation, the United States showed interest in a Jewish Palestine aside from religious motives. For instance, in a not so well known story, when a significant portion of Palestine's Jews in the first World War were forced to flee the land, an American gunboat took refugees to Alexandria in northern Egypt. In the same year, when food was scarce in the Holy Land, the American government sponsored shipments of food. A ship called the Vulcan was sent to Palestine, along with two American Jewish Zionists, to feed the Jews. Turkey, who controlled Palestine, was even warned by the United States that any massacre or harm (including property loss) aimed at either Jews or Christians would be held accountable.[26]

President Wilson was in some respects a supporter of Jewish and Zionist causes. His appointment of Louis Brandeis to the Supreme Court in 1916, the first Jew to sit on the court, was a milestone. Undoubtedly, Brandeis influenced Wilson in a multitude of policies and initiatives, including in regards to Zionism.[27] Before the Balfour Declaration, Wilson showed signs of Zionist support. For instance, it was reported in numerous daily newspapers, that on April 14, 1917, six months before the issuance of the Balfour Declaration, Wilson would meet Balfour in what was termed the "Balfour Mission," and among other things to be discussed, was the issue of creating of a Jewish state in Palestine.

The next day, on April 15, the Provisional Executive Committee for General Zionist Affairs released to the press some of the information that was proclaimed by Sir Archibald Murray, who had, via his military maneuvering, reached Gaza. Murray's view was released to the press. "What should be done with Palestine thus liberated from the centuries old Turkish grip? There can be little doubt that we should revive the Jewish Palestine of old, and allow the Jews to realize their dream of Zion in their homeland."[28] It should be noticed that April 15, when the bulletin went out to the press about the upcoming meeting, that six months would pass before the issuance of the Balfour Declaration. Murray's comments resulted in mixed reactions, yet for the most part most newspapers reacted positively to the idea to the creation of a Jewish national home. In the following six months, the favorable American view of a Jewish homeland would help pave the way for both the British to issue the Balfour Declaration in November, as well as foment American state-sponsored support for Zionism over the coming years. Eventually, the United States would create its own Balfour-type declaration.

Newspapers, journals, and religious periodicals help shed significant light upon national sentiments and many such publications discussed the pros and cons of the creation of a Jewish homeland in Palestine. In regards to the Balfour Declaration, a majority of American publications viewed the British proclamation as positive. Although some feared that the Jews would leave the United States en mass if a Jewish state was created, for the most part it was generally believed that the masses of Jews would remain where they were. However, newspaper editorials such New York's *Evening Globe*, the *Leavenworth Times* and the *Richmond Journal*, among others, asserted that "the remnant that has survived centuries of oppression will find freedom in a restored Jewish homeland."[29] In both the *Dayton* (Ohio) *News* and the *Kansas City Times*, which the latter city became a hub for Zionist support in the early 1920s, as will be shown, both surmised that one not assume that the Jews themselves are united on the Zionist endeavor. To the contrary, they asserted, Zionism and the Balfour Declaration have left the Jews almost in disarray.[30] Some editorials surmised that practicing Christians, and eventually the Christian world, will lend their support for the "recreation of Israel."[31] The *Patterson* (New Jersey) *Guardian* asks: "What could be more fitting than a Jewish nation reborn after centuries of travail? A Jewish Republic? Why not?"[32] The *Waterloo* (Iowa) *Courier* declared that a Jewish state will be created and that "no crusader would have considered such a disposition of the Holy Land, but we are more tolerant today."[33]

This American "tolerance" was indeed played out in the press. In fact, two common themes can be found throughout the rhetoric of Christian supporters of Zionism: 1) That the Jews are the Chosen People, or that Jesus was a Jew and therefore to hasten the redemption of the world the Jews must re-congregate in the Holy Land. All of this translates into Christian messianism, and; 2) that a historic justice would be meted out to the Jews for all of the calamities, in the name of Christianity, that befell them throughout their centuries of exile. Helping the Jews reacquire the Holy Land could partially rectify nearly 2,000 years of Christian misdeeds. The editor of the New York City *Continent* wrote that "After all the centuries of persecution...committed against the Jews in the name of Jesus, what a glory it will be...to make reparations in a great international kindness."[34]

Other editorials asserted that the creation of a Jewish state would solve "the Jewish problem." This "problem" though, had many different facets, including such issues as Jewish refugees and assimilation. The former could be solved if the Jews had a state of their own, yet the latter, that of assimilating, should not be encouraged by Christians. The Denver (Colorado) *Times* editorialized that Jewish assimilation would not solve the problem of the Jews. "You cannot solve the problem of the Jewish nation by inviting it to assimilate utterly and disappear...it would be a great loss to the world if it could." With that in mind, the Denver *Times* endorsed the Balfour Declaration.[35]

Other newspapers supported the Balfour Declaration for idealistic or romantic notions, while some believed it would be practical for the world powers if the Jews had a state of their own. While most editorials discussed the aforementioned, few references to the issue of dual loyalty were dealt with. However, those that dedicated space to this question generally dismissed the dual loyalty charge as "absurd" or "nonsense."[36] The Memphis, Tennessee *Appeal* stated that

> some Jews are timorous about declaring devotion to Zionism because they fear their allegiance to a country where they may be questioned. No sane Jew would draw such conclusions.[37]

For those Jews that the Memphis *Appeal* would call "insane" for believing that supporting Zionism constituted dual loyalty, the only major newspaper with such misgivings was the Jewish-owned *The New York Times*. A cautionary approach was taken by the *Times*, for the fear was that open Jewish support for the Balfour Declaration would eventually spawn anti-Semitism, most notably stemming from the charges of multiple national loyalties. In fact, from the Balfour Declaration of November 1917 through the Palestine Lodge-Fish Resolution of September 1922, *The New York Times* took an anti-Zionist position. Articles debunking the movement and the endeavor could be consistently found on its editorial pages.[38]

The opposition of *The New York Times* notwithstanding, with support from some newspapers around the country – there was opposition as well – the Zionist movement found important allies in the quest for statehood. Numerous periodicals and magazines debated the merits of the Balfour Declaration and the potential future Jewish state. The American Jewish Congress was portrayed in the popular journal, the *Survey*, as "glowing" in joy from the Balfour Declaration.[39] Yet earlier that year, in an article in the *New Republic*, strife was predicted to be commonplace between the Jews and the Arabs of Palestine. In a follow up article one year later by Morris Cohen, a Jew, it was maintained that Zionism was not a solution to the Jewish problem. Morris alleged that the creation of a Jewish state was predicated on the fact that such a belief of "…race, a tribal religion and a mystic belief in a peculiar soil" was immensely un-American, especially in regards to the separation of Church and State.[40] In the *Atlantic Monthly*, a grave warning was issued in case the Jews do not make Palestine into a Jewish majority.

> Unless this is done…and the country becomes full of Russian, Roumanian and Polish Jews, so that they will be in a majority… anti-Semitism will be intensified to a greater degree than now exists.[41]

The Zionists, however, countered such claims and stated that the Jews would one day be the majority population if only the British would stop its policy of maintaining a Jewish minority. This sentiment was somewhat echoed by Christians in their support of Zionism. By early 1920, many Christian groups had become practical supporters of Zionism and vowed to combat anti-Zionist forces, if they be found, with any political, social or economic means possible. This is mainly true of the dominant Protestant branches of Christianity, where at a luncheon in early 1920 at the Zionist Organization of America (ZOA) 141 clergymen pledged their support to the Zionist movement.[42]

It was understood by mainstream Protestant groups that a Jewish return to the land of Israel will precede the second coming of Christ. It is this core belief that still allows for Protestant support of Zionism. However, it should be added that numerous Christian groups from various denominations were also excited for a Jewish return to the Holy Land, as it would, they believed, facilitate their conversion to Christianity sooner rather than later.[43]

The popular Catholic journal, *The Month*, was antagonistic towards the Balfour Declaration and Zionism in particular, as well as other

Christian groups that supported both. *The Month* feared that if the Jews took over the Holy Land injustices against the Arab and Christian inhabitants of the land would be commonplace.[44] It was even argued – not just by Catholics – that Biblical prophecy should not be invoked in order to support the Balfour Declaration. The Presbyterian journal the *Continent*, among other arguments opposed to a Jewish state, also asserted that prophecy was not a sure guide in such political affairs. Furthermore, one need not even look to prophecy for the pitfalls of Zionism, as the Jews themselves, they argued, are bitterly divided in regards to Jewish nationalism. The *Continent*, in support of their view, quoted a verdict from the Central Conference of American Rabbis, the Reform Movement's rabbinical body: "Israel is not a nation but a religious community. Palestine is not the homeland for the Jewish people, the whole world aught to be their home."[45]

This view was supported on various occasions by Henry Morgenthau, a prominent Reform leader and a US Ambassador to the Ottoman Empire. He was vehemently opposed to Zionism. For years his name was invoked by anti-Zionists to disclaim the merits of the Balfour Declaration and Zionism altogether. Morgenthau wrote that

> Zionism is the most stupendous folly in Jewish history – politically unjust…spiritually sterile; economically unsound; socially provocative of the very menace from which the Jews are trying to liberate themselves.

Based on Morgenthau's views, the *Christian Century*, in an article by Herbert Willet, concluded that "The occupation of Palestine by Jews would require the expulsion of its rightful possessors…Palestine is wholly unfitted by location, character and extent, to be the home of the modern Jew."[46] This argument was followed by stating that the Orthodox Jews of Jerusalem do not support the endeavor either.[47]

Generally speaking, various Jewish groups, denominations and individuals reacted differently to the Balfour Declaration. For some Jews, Balfour was a pseudo Jewish savior, similar to Persia's King Cyrus, and his declaration a culmination of hundreds of years of prayer.[48] Some went as far as to claim that the Balfour Declaration was "the greatest occurrence in modern Jewish history."[49] As noted, though, Reform publications (the Reform Movement was the largest Jewish denomination in the US at the time) were quick to denounce the Balfour Declaration, including opposing the view that it was the greatest Jewish achievement of the modern period. However, something changed within many of the anti-Zionists Jews following a letter by President Wilson openly endorsing the Balfour Declaration. Wilson wrote a letter to Rabbi Stephen Wise, the head of the Reform Movement, sanctioning the Balfour Declaration and all of its ramifications, placing many Jews who were aloof to Zionism in an uncomfortable, defensive position. Wilson wrote that

> I welcome an opportunity to express the satisfaction I have felt in the progress of the Zionist movement in the United States and in the allied countries since the declaration of Mr. Balfour, on behalf of the British Government, of Great Britain's approval of the establishment in Palestine of a national home for the Jewish people and his promise that the British Government would use its best endeavors to facilitate the achievement of that object, with the understanding that nothing would be done to prejudice the civil and religious rights of non-Jewish people in Palestine or the rights and political status enjoyed by Jews in other countries."[50]

Wilson's statement was read by Congressman Hamilton Fish in 1922 while giving testimony in front of Congress regarding the issuance of a Congressional pro-Zionist resolution. Fish, as will be shown later, was a strong supporter of such a pro-Zionist resolution. He, in fact, sponsored the resolution in the House of Representative.[51]

The letter also impacted those Jews who called themselves "non-Zionists." Claiming neither support for nor antagonism of Zionism, many of the leaders of American Jewry, particularly at the American Jewish Committee would also have a change of heart. Most of these leaders were affiliated with Reform Judaism, but as the years moved on many became less antagonistic towards Zionism, nay even staunch supporters.[52] Following the Balfour Declaration, Reform was forced on the defensive for their cold sentiments regarding Zionism, claiming that they weren't opposed to Jews (especially Jewish refugees) colonizing Palestine, just that no nationalistic sentiments be expressed. On the contrary, they argued, Reform and the so called "non-Zionists" gave money to the Keren Hayasod (a major body dedicated to building up the Jewish presence in Palestine), helped in the creation of the Hebrew University in Jerusalem which opened in 1925, and lobbied the British when they felt they had overstepped their boundaries in regards to the

Palestine Mandate.[53]

In the Yiddish papers, most viewed with favor the Balfour Declaration, and some even attacked those that opposed Zionism. The Orthodox daily, *Dos Yiddishe Tageblatt*, asserted that the Balfour Declaration was cause for celebration, and in a later issue eulogized Theodor Herzl, and stated that President Wilson's letter to Rabbi Wise pledging his support of Zionism, issued on the eve of Rosh Hashanah, was "a New Years present" to all the Jews.[54] The largest Yiddish paper, the *Forvertz* (Forward), which was socialist in its orientation, made no comment for the first two weeks after the Balfour Declaration was issued. The paper surmised that the declaration was made in the interest of money, for such notable banker-businessmen as the Rothchilds and Jacob H. Schiff made it clear that Jewish financing and ultimately Jewish monetary profit was the sole reason that these Jews both supported and lobbied for its passing. Essentially, this was a blatant disregard for the truth.[55]

Many of the Yiddish readers were socialist, and gave little ear for anything other than the ideals of socialism.[56] Nevertheless, stern opposition to Zionism came from the extreme left and right of the Jews. Reform opposed Zionism because they asserted the Jews as a nation have since vanished, and Washington and America could serve just as well as Jerusalem and Israel. Orthodox opposition, however, had two distinct reasons for either their cool response to Zionism, or their outright rejection of it. Most well known is the Orthodox repudiation of secular Jews leading such a movement. Only a Jewry dedicated to the Torah, it was argued, will bring about Jewish redemption. However opposed to Zionism many Orthodox Jews were because of the Zionist leadership's irreligiousness, many opposed Zionism because of the injunctions found in the Talmudic tractate of *Ketuvot* (111a), where the *Shelosh Shavuot*, the Three Oaths, are discussed. God, according to the Talmud "forced" or "imposed" on the Jewish people three oaths or obligations upon entering the exile in the years following the destruction of the Temple in Jerusalem, which occurred in the year 70 CE.

- Oath #1: Israel (the people) is not to "ascend" or "storm" the land of Israel like a "wall" (essentially not to take control of the land by force);
- Oath #2: Israel is not to "rebel" against the nations of the world;
- Oath #3: That the nations of the world not excessively oppress

the Jewish people (this oath was directed at the non-Jewish nations).

Although not the place for an in-depth discussion of the Three Oaths or the varying interpretations by rabbinic scholars over the centuries, or their significance during the early Zionist period up until today, they did play a central role in many in Orthodoxy's opposition or cold reception to Zionism. For many other Orthodox Jews, the Oaths were not accepted as binding or they did not have any *halakhic* (Jewish law) relevance.[57] It should be added, though, that a significant portion of Orthodoxy supported the Zionist cause, including the Mizrahi movement which will be discussed elsewhere. Many in Orthodoxy understood that if a Jewish state was created, it would eventually follow the dictates of the Torah and be the conduit for the redemption of Israel.[58]

The Reform's anti-Zionist position had been clear from the inception of the Zionist movement and only gained strength as the political happenings, particularly the Balfour Declaration, intensified. Although the Reform movement would issue such anti-Zionist statements following the Balfour Declaration, they were, in spirit, statements made by its leaders. Very few negative practical affects resulted from their remarks. It would not be until the years 1920-1922 that the Reform movement, as will be illustrated, would undertake such initiatives as to literally attempt to thwart United States government support of Zionism, even appearing before Congressional committees to argue the "untruth" that the Jews constitute a nation.

Nevertheless, following the Balfour Declaration, the Central Conference of American Rabbis, the rabbinic arm of Reform, again passed a resolution dispelling the idea that the Jews are in fact a national entity.

> We herewith affirm the fundamental principles of Reform Judaism that the essence of Israel, as a Priest People, consists in its religious consciousness...and not in any political or racial national consciousness.[59]

As it has been pointed out though, Reform opposition to the Balfour Declaration and Zionism did not reach the masses of the American press. The opposition, as opposed to the year 1922, was mainly conducted from the synagogue pulpit and various Reform or anti-Zionist publications.[60]

However, in one glaring instance where anti-Zionist Jews tried to persuade President Wilson to abandon his Zionist position caused quite a commotion. In 1919, on his way to the Paris Peace Conference (where the Allies decided how to proceed with the aftermath of World War I, notably the former territories of the Ottoman Empire) Wilson was given a letter signed by some 299 "prominent" Jews, which included, among many other notables, Henry Morgenthau and Adolph Ochs, the publisher of *The New York Times*. The letter basically stated that the Jews do not constitute a separate nation, and because of that reason, neither require nor desire a separate state. The statement was handed to the President by Congressman Julius Kahn, on March 4, 1919, and appeared the next day, on the 5th, in *The New York Times*.[61]

President Wilson did not accept the letter with enthusiasm nor did he find any merit in Jewish opposition to Zionism. Rabbi Stephen Wise wrote the following:

> The writer remembers, in a moment of great anxiety, to have asked President Wilson: "What will you do if a protest reaches you signed by many of the outstanding American Jews?" The President made no verbal answer. He merely pointed to his waste basket, and said grimly: "Don't you think that waste basket is large enough to contain a protest by any Jew who may be opposed to a Jewish Palestine?"[62]

Echoing the Reform position in regards to Zionism, though in a different vein, was the American State Department, a government body that over the course of its existence has treated the movement rather coldly. Right up until the creation of the State of Israel, the State Department impeded the Jews' attempt at reconverting Palestine into a Jewish state. Although the Department of State eventually supported President Harding's decision to support Zionism in 1922, following the Balfour Declaration, however, there was no such encouragement emanating from its leaders. Yet President Wilson was unfaltering in his buttress of Zionism (at least verbally), even to the opposition of the State Department and many prominent American Jews.

Right around the same time as the letter of 299 Jews made its way to Wilson, the President was busy meeting with a delegation of the American Jewish Congress (March 2, 1919). In this meeting Wilson again conferred his support for the Balfour Declaration, even though some in the room rejected Jewish claims of nationalism.[63]

As for your representations touching Palestine, I have before this expressed my personal approval for the declaration of the British Government regarding the aspirations and historic claims of the Jewish people in regard to Palestine. I am, moreover, persuaded that the Allied nations, with the fullest concurrence of our government and people, are agreed that in Palestine shall be laid the foundations of a Jewish commonwealth.[64]

Of course, however, the State Department did not view such statements as binding, or as an official American endorsement of Zionism. Yet the Zionists had found a consistent verbal supporter of the movement at the very top of the American government. No opposition either by the State Department, Reform Jews, or non-Zionists, would deter Wilson. On January 21, 1919, at the Paris Peace Conference, one of the first of many public American endorsements for the creation of a Jewish state was expressed. The recommendations of the Commission were as follows:

It is recommended that there be established a separate state of Palestine. It is recommended that this state be placed under Great Britain as mandatory of the League of Nations. It is recommended that the Jews be invited to return to Palestine and settle there, being assured by the Conference of all proper assistance in so doing that may be consistent with the protection of the personal and property rights of the non-Jewish population and being further assured that it will be the policy of the League of Nations to recognize Palestine as a Jewish state as soon as it is a Jewish state in fact.

The report then concluded:

It is right that Palestine should become a Jewish state…It was the cradle and home of their vital race…and is the only land in which they can hope to find a home of their own.[65]

While the President's support upset various government and non-government bodies, the United States Congress looked favorably upon the White House endorsement of the Balfour Declaration in general and Zionism's goal in particular. The Balfour Declaration, therefore, was received with delight by many in Congress. In June 1918, 69 senators representing 43 states, and 231 members of the House of Representatives representing 44 states, openly approved Balfour's recommendations.[66]

Many congressmen supported Zionism for various reasons, yet two features once again stand out: Historic justice for a homeless people, and Christian messianism. Opinion polls and voting blocs may have been small factors in some localities but playing to the Jewish vote was not a main reason for support – justice for the Jews and messianic overtones played the largest role for non-Jewish, Christian support of Zionism – both in the British Balfour Declaration of 1917, and later with the numerous Palestine resolutions subsequently passed in the United States Congress and signed by the President.

The Zionist Movement Post World War I

The Zionist movement post World War I was in distress. The political leaders of Zionism were at odds with each other, mostly due to the vision and long term goals of the movement. For instance, Chaim Weizmann, the British statesman and leader of the Zionist movement asserted that all necessary means – and therefore all resources – be gravitated to the ideals of Jewish nationalism. Thus, Zionism should climax with the founding of a Jewish state. Separately was Louis Brandeis, also a leader of Zionism – although his time was mainly focused on his newly appointed position on the US Supreme Court – believed that the building up of the *Yishuv*, the Jewish community in Palestine, should commence, but that nationalism should not be the goal, at least at the present time. He felt that resources could be better utilized elsewhere such as in the expanded immigration of Jews to Palestine, assisting Jewish refugees in Europe and developing better infrastructure in Palestine such as roads and hospitals. Both had practical applications for the Zionist movement, but this disagreement eventually became the "great schism" in post-World War I Zionism, literally splitting the movement in two. This schism, however, led to a chain of events that ended in a positive note in the White House. These dual visions came about after Zionism, just two years prior, had been given a more prominent role on the European scene with the issuance of the Balfour Declaration.

Following the historic passing of the Balfour Declaration by the British Parliament on November 2, 1917, the Zionist movement was infused with new life.[67] Although still viewed by many in the Zionist and Jewish world as a far off dream, Balfour recognized – and in many ways legitimized – the centrality of the historic connection of the Jewish people to the land of Israel. It became British policy to support the creation of a "Jewish national home", and while this "home" was neither defined as a Jewish state or commonwealth by the declaration, it was viewed by many a Zionist and Parliamentarian as the precursor affirmation of an independent, national Jewish state.

The Balfour Declaration was the Zionist movement's greatest accomplishment since the convening of the first Zionist Congress in 1897. Following the Basel Conference and until Herzl's untimely death in 1904, the movement had gained steady momentum and popularly increased among Jews worldwide. With the absence of

Herzl, however, Zionism weakened to the point that by World War I the rank and file of Zionist followers diminished, as did the funding. Much though would change with the outcome of the war. With the defeat of the Turks in 1916, England and France would carve up lands of the former Ottoman Empire. The Sykes-Picot Agreement divided conquered Ottoman lands, where England took control of Palestine and Trans-Jordan, while Syria and Lebanon was apportioned to France.[68]

With the overthrowing of the Turks in Palestine, the Zionist movement, it was felt, had found a much less antagonistic entity with the British.[69] It was considered in the Zionist movement that a British victory in the war would greatly enhance the chances of attaining at least a portion of ancestral Jewish land. With the Turks, however, many in the movement had consistently been discouraged with Ottoman rhetoric and actions. For instance, even though Zionism was not a powerful movement at the turn of the 20th Century, the Ottoman Empire, fearing that Zionism could become a threat, slowly revoked certain Jewish privileges. Most notably, the Turks restricted Jewish immigration and land transfers to Jews who were not from the Ottoman Empire.[70] Although the Ottomans attempted to quell Zionism, it had little effect. Ottoman Jews were permitted to visit Palestine either for business or pilgrimage. By 1901, even many Jews who entered illegally would eventually be granted permanent resident rights by legal loopholes. The easing of restrictions was similar for land transfers. Arab landowners who wished to sell their property found Jews more than willing to purchase from them. Additionally, intermediaries and the interference of foreign consuls allowed Jews to purchase land even though they were "illegal residents".

There is little evidence to suggest that the Turks were opposed to Zionism due to anti-Semitic sentiments. The Ottoman dilemma was mainly political, which the British inherited. By the late 19th Century the Ottoman Empire faced two concerning problems: nationalist and secessionist movements. Turkish authorities feared that such ideological movements would weaken their empire. In particular, Zionist settlement would exacerbate these issues. The fear, of course, was that if Zionism succeeded it would create a nation – possibly with a Jewish minority – that would be located in a hostile, strategic region. Thus, Ottoman influence would cease. Some Turkish officials compared this imbroglio to nationalistic movements of Macedonia or Armenia, which evidently weakened the Ottoman Empire both strategically and politically.[71] As history has shown, Turkish fears in regards to Zionism were not without reason.[72]

During the war, the Turkish government intensified its campaign against Zionism. Arab nationalism that swept across the Arab world in the latter quarter of the 19th Century would by World War I force the Ottomans to place additional restrictions on Jews.[73] Zionist associations were barred in Palestine and many leaders were deported from the country. During the war, approximately 11,000 Jews left Palestine for other countries.[74] However, an outcome of WWI was that the Turks were conquered and finished in Palestine. The Zionist movement was about to be altered.

It took more than a year of secret negotiations between Zionist leaders and members of the British government to secure an English declaration in favor of a Jewish national home. The Balfour Declaration, though, was viewed by many, particularly the Arab world, and to a certain extent by France, as an abrogation of prior British commitments, the first being the McMahon Letter of October 24, 1915. In correspondence with Hussein Ali, Sharif of Mecca, Sir Henry McMahon, High Commissioner of Cairo, promised Sharif Hussein a pan-Arab state that stretched from the Persian Gulf to the Mediterranean, with Sharif Hussein, of course, as the head of this massive nation.[75]

Almost simultaneous to the McMahon Letter, another secret treaty was transpiring between England and France, notably the eventual Sykes-Picot Agreement of May 1916. In this treaty, among other statutes, England promised France the territory of Syria in return for their help in ridding the Middle East of the Turks. The problem however, was that England had already promised Syria to Sharif Hussein of Mecca. Although France eventually was informed of the British promise to Sharif Hussein, three years of negotiations were undertaken between the two nations. Yet by 1919, at the Paris Peace Conference, France basically withdrew from Sykes-Picot, as Syria was by then overrun by the Sharif's men, and the French could see very little hope of a British clean up.

The last of the three secret agreements, the Balfour Declaration, angered both the French and the Arabs, yet pleased the Zionists.[76] Nevertheless, following the declaration, many downplayed its significance, including many Jews. In fact, the wording of the declaration went through several versions prior to being finalized, as many wanted clarification as to just what was meant by a "Jewish national home."[77] Regardless of the semantic, a national home had been called for, inculcating the Zionist movement. The dream of a Jewish national home, though for many far off, was becoming one step closer to fruition.[78]

Yet even though England promised some form of Jewish independence, the Zionist movement would not be permitted to rest. On the contrary, the "easy" part was out of the way, now more practical measures such as Jewish immigration and the continued sustenance and growth of the *Yishuv* (the Jewish community of Palestine) took on new meaning. If able bodies could not be counted among the majority of Palestine's population – and even if they were a minority – international support for a Jewish homeland would be minimal to none if the Jewish community there showed little promise for growth and sustainability.

The issue of able bodies was understood by many to mean the Jewish refugees, which took center stage following World War I. As the Zionist movement faced increasing budgetary crises which put the movement at the brink of bankruptcy, American Jewry would be called upon to rescue practical Zionism. Although many leaders of the movement understood that the masses of American Jewry would never make the arduous choice to live in their ancient homeland, it was believed that at the very least they could supplement the costs of those who chose to.[79] In and out of British Parliament, the Zionists both lobbied and pleaded for England to make good on their promise.

The *Yishuv*, however, aside from its political and economic development, was being dictated by outside forces, namely now the British, who had been granted international recognition as the mandate holder of Palestine in the San Remo Conference of 1920. Even though England officially controlled the mandate, unrest in Palestine became almost commonplace, particularly beginning in the early 1920s where rioting engulfed parts of the country. Subsequent to an outburst of riots during 1920-1921, the Haycraft Commission that Britain assigned to investigate the happenings warned that Jewish immigration was the main catalyst behind Arab discomfort, which ultimately led to the riots.[80] Thus, Zionism took another blow in the June 2, 1922 Churchill White Paper, issued in response to Arab reaction to the Jewish community's "usurping" the land, which led to the enactment of the first of numerous immigration restrictions to come, called "White Papers". Many viewed this first British White Paper as a reneging of its commitments in the Balfour Declaration.[81]

On top of British placation, the Zionist movement, though still overtly enthused since Balfour, had begun to show ideological and practical differences. Internal fighting, particularly in the American Zionist scene, led to the virtual severing of ties between the two most important figures in Zionism, Chaim Weizmann and Louis Brandeis. Fundamental differences on what direction the movement should take, as well as how Jewish American funds should be spent on Zionism, split the two.[82] So deep was this schism that Weizmann and Brandeis stopped communication and each eventually founded a new centralized Zionist movement of his own. "Pinsk versus Washington," it was popularly alleged (including by Weizmann), or "East versus West."[83]

On the one hand, Weizmann was the statesman who could claim that it was European Jews who were making the arduous choice to live in Palestine, therefore, they (and their leadership) should decide how to disperse funds. Brandeis, on the other, who for several years by this point sat on the United States Supreme Court and had thus resigned his official post in the Zionist movement, believed that those who financed the majority of Zionist endeavors, i.e. American Jews, should have the final say where the monies are directed.

The leadership of the movement however, fell into the hands of Weizmann, who was elected President of the World Zionist Organization (WZO) at the Zionist Conference in London in July 1920. Brandeis, reluctant and embittered by Weizmann's ascension to the WZO leadership, agreed to serve an Honorary President within the movement, though the quarrel between the two only intensified. The battle between the two can be highlighted by the acutest issue at hand, which was what direction the movement should pursue. For Brandeis, all political aspirations of the Zionist movement, i.e. the quest for statehood, had ended with the proclamation of the Balfour Declaration and England's grasping of the Mandate. Henceforth, he argued, the movement should only pursue constructive work in Palestine and leave the political process alone. Weizmann diametrically opposed this view and believed that simultaneous to the constructive work, all political muscle and influence should be marshaled specifically for convincing the British (and later the Americans) that the Balfour Declaration be implemented to the fullest political extent. The Jews, he argued, should push for a Jewish state.

The Brandeis-Weizmann schism also centered around 25 million British Pounds held by the Keren Hayasod, the Palestine Foundation Fund created in 1920 at the London Zionist Conference. How to disperse these funds triggered an intense and unfortunate outcome. The Brandeis camp asserted that the monies should be spent, as noted, only on development projects, while Weizmann opted for both *Yishuv* expansion as well as political objectives.[84] In addition, Zionist leaders ultimately disagreed on two main issues regarding the funds, namely 1) who would control the money; and 2) would the contributions be placed into a general fund for all Zionist undertakings in Palestine or only to be used for public services. Furthermore, if the latter was agreed upon, would separate investment corporations be created for additional expenditures?

Brandeis preferred the business approach much more so than Weizmann. He therefore advocated separate funds for differing objectives. After all, he reasoned, the majority of donations would be coming from his constituency, American Jewry.[85] He insisted that his group or the local American federations control the fund(s), not the World Zionist Executive. Particularly, he wanted the Zionist Organization of America (ZOA), the largest US Zionist group, to make the major decisions of the Zionist movement and disburse the funds, something Weizmann vehemently opposed.[86]

In a meeting with the British statesmen Lloyd George (who was Prime Minister) and Arthur Balfour in 1921, Weizmann later wrote that both Brits were in agreement that the Balfour Declaration called for an eventual Jewish state.[87] It was Weizmann's understanding that other British politicians shared the same view as George and Balfour. However, over the course of two years, from June 1920 through June 1922, the Palestine Mandate, a document slated to be sent by the British to the League of Nations for approval, went through no less than three drafts, each with differing conclusions in regards to a "Jewish national home." This led to great discomfort throughout the Zionist movement.[88]

Weizmann was most distressed over the various struggles. In several of his letters written at this time one can easily discern his feelings in regard to those who attempted to thwart the Zionist movement. Weizmann was openly angry at such antagonists, even for those politicians who felt they were pursuing a proper or moral course. For instance, among others beside the British, the Brandeis camp was often target of Weizmann's wrath. Weizmann wanted all Zionist funds – that is, the Keren Hayasod – under one executive branch, where he felt that the common cause would be better served as one cohesive unit rather than different branches supporting their arbitrary choice of development.

The Brandeis-Weizmann schism was almost inventible due to

both camps' social and ideological outlooks. Weizmann's camp consisted mainly of those Jews from the *shtetls*, clearly poorer than their brethren in America, yet strikingly more Jewish in both life and culture. Brandeis's followers were mainly those born in the United States, particularly both the large donors as well as the leadership of Zionism. The difference in culture was so glaring that Weizmann, often disillusioned with Brandeis and his camp, clearly spelled out his feelings:

> He (Brandeis) is so un-Jewish in his outlook, in his feelings, and has never attempted to realize the deep causes which have moved the Jewish masses towards Palestine. He is a colonizer purely and simply. He happens to colonize Palestine.[89]

Such statements of ridicule became more common. Weizmann was apt to call Brandeis's Jewish view "Yankee Doodle Judaism," and labeled his camp as "plain Americans" who are "rule oriented, dogmatic, materialistic, calculating, and, above all, cold."[90]

Following the Zionist Conference in London, two other gatherings highlighted the differences between Brandeis and Weizmann. At a November 1920 WZO convention in Buffalo, New York, and again in April 1921, the London Conference that a year earlier had adopted Weizmann's approach toward practical and political Zionism had agreed this time that Brandies's approach was more suitable. Weizmann, of course, protested the directives and warned that Zionism was on the cusp of destruction. After months of haggling with the Brandeis camp, Weizmann, on April 17, 1921, announced at a WZO meeting that he was creating the Keren Hayasod as he saw fit, sidestepping the Brandeis camp. Shortly after, he began appealing directly to American Jews for support.[91]

Two months later, in June, at a Zionist conference in Cleveland, Weizmann again trumped Brandeis and his supporters. The delegates overwhelmingly approved the Weizmann approach to Zionism, and following this fateful assembly Brandeis would never again acquire the Zionist leadership nor would he dictate the agenda of the movement.[92] In response, Brandeis resigned as Honorary President of the World Zionist Organization and founded a fund to rival the Keren Hayasod, the Palestine Devolvement Associates. The outcome of the conference evidently weakened Zionism, specifically in regards to raising funds. Yet it also promised to keep Zionism under one unified branch with a centralized authority.[93] Even though it appeared that the Zionist movement would stay intact and that events on the ground in Palestine – from the demise of Ottoman rule to British promises of a Jewish homeland – much work remained. Current events dictated that Zionism continue its course and in many respects begin a more aggressive campaign to secure a Jewish homeland in Palestine.

At the Cleveland Conference Weizmann would begin the next phase of the Zionist movement's goal by commissioning Rabbi Simon Glazer to assist. Weizmann asked Glazer, who at the time was a leading rabbi of the small Jewish community in Kansas City, Missouri to lead a lobbying campaign to convince the US government to go on record supporting the Balfour Declaration. He was, in essence, asked to lobby both Houses of Congress and the President of the United States. Thus, not only was the Cleveland Conference so pivotal in regards to the future of the Zionist Executive and how Zionist funds would be dispersed, but it also became a moment in Zionist history that would prove significant. Even though at the Cleveland Conference the movement was split in two and therefore weakened Zionism, it also shaped much of the Zionist agenda that lay ahead.

The Cleveland Conference And Weizmann's Unorthodox Choice

The commissioning of Rabbi Simon Glazer to lobby various government branches and politicians to support Zionism is quite perplexing. Although Glazer was familiar with many of the leaders of American Jewry, he was not a politician, nor did he strive to be. Furthermore, Glazer was so far removed from the politics of Washington – not just geographically – that for many it appeared that his services could permanently damage, or at the very least set back, the Zionist movement's goal of achieving American government support of Zionism. Rabbi Glazer, a pious Orthodox Jew, was born in a small town in Lithuania. For years he served small town Jewish communities and avoided political struggles. As a man with little lobbying experience and few contacts in Washington, D.C., Weizmann still asserted that Glazer was the correct choice to lead such a campaign. Some historical background as to why Glazer would be asked to lead such an important mission, however, needs to be explained.

As noted, following the Brandeis-Weizmann schism the Zionist movement split in two. From the point of view of the Brandeis camp, it was Weizmann and his group that had been sidestepping the American Zionist federations, ultimately leading to the split. From Weizmann's perspective, American Jewish leaders were not interested in seriously achieving the creation of a Jewish state, which had led Weizmann to conclude that he should form his own movement if Zionism is to survive. Although elected to the head of the World Zionist Organization at the London Conference of 1920, while Brandeis became the Honorary President, the battles between the two only intensified, almost climaxing with the Zionist conference of April 17, 1921 in Buffalo, New York, and lastly in Cleveland, Ohio in June 1921 with the splitting of the movement.

Yet internal fighting between the two camps took some time to foster. In January 1921 many leaders of American Zionism resigned their positions within the movement, mostly to protest Weizmann's policies. Then, when the April conference arrived and Weizmann's team endeavored to create a new Keren Hayasod (a fund where money for Zionism was donated and dispersed), more resignations were forthcoming. Both Weizmann and Brandeis though, did not want to isolate members from either party so that American Zionism would crumble. Therefore, both sides tried to avoid a complete breakdown of the movement by attempting to bridge their differences. One of Brandeis's main allies was Judge Julian Mack (who held various US District Court seats) who, on more than one occasion, met with Weizmann in order to end the dissension. Initially, Weizmann and Mack made progress in this endeavor, particularly in regards to the Keren Hayasod where the two agreed that the Zionist Organization of America would spend all funds in Palestine.[94]

Weizmann named a four person commission, which was tasked to draft a provisional agreement that would last until the forthcoming Zionist Congressional meeting in September 1921. After reviewing the commission's recommendations, however, Weizmann believed that the agreement would hinder the Zionist movement's objectives. Therefore, he rejected any of the Brandeis camp proposals and henceforth opened the new Keren Hayasod fund.

Simultaneous to the creation of the Keren Hayasod, other leaders in the American Zionist scene began to openly question the Brandeis camp agenda. Two such individuals, who would, in the following year, come to play a significant role in the lobbying of various government officials on behalf of Zionism, were Louis Lipsky, the Secretary General of the Zionist Organization of America, and Abraham Goldberg, Secretary of the Palestine Bureau (and member of the Administrative Committee of the ZOA). Both individuals had been allies of Brandeis, but once the inevitable split between Weizmann and Brandeis transpired, they became closer to the "Pinsk" agenda, particularly in regards to the goal of creating a Jewish national home. Indeed, both asserted that Weizmann's path was more logical and that Jewish statehood should materialize. Lipsky even founded and became the first editor of *The New Palestine*, a paper dedicated to the support of Keren Hayasod.[95]

All of this played an important role in the American Jewish Congress's 24th convention in Cleveland in June 1921, where a vote of "no confidence" in the leadership of the Zionist movement passed. As a consequence, such notable American Zionist figures such as Justice Brandies, Judge Mack, Rabbis Stephen Wise and Abba Hillel Silver and Prof. Felix Frankfurter (later to be Supreme Court Justice), as well as 32 other members of the National Executive Committee resigned their positions in the movement. On June 19, 1921 Brandeis tendered his resignation as the Honorary President of the World Zionist Organization, a position, as noted, he would never again acquire.[96]

Weizmann, echoing the mood of the movement, asserted that "There is no bridge between Washington and Pinsk".[97]

Many leaders of American Jewry (as well as Zionism) feared that without Brandeis or his camp Zionist support would falter. As the American Jewish face of Zionism, Brandeis had been welcomed by those American Jews as a "mini savior." It was even observed by Brandeis's biographer that when he gave his famous speech in support of Zionism in Boston's Symphony Hall, "the corridors were filled with cries of 'the New Moses, the New Moses.'"[98] His message would be reiterated for many years to come. Particularly, his message would be immortalized at future Zionist meetings. "To be better Americans we must become better Jews, and to be better Jews we must become better Zionists."[99]

With a loss of such a prominent face, Zionism indeed appeared greatly fractured. The Pinsk followers, as noted earlier by Weizmann, believed that a rift between East and West was inevitable and even mandatory for the movement to proceed. Weizmann and his people presented themselves as men of vision, infused with *Yiddishkeit*, while the American delegates were inculcated with Gentile culture. One of Weizmann's associates asserted that "Americans had *goyische kops* (gentile heads, which had a negative connotation) whereas the Eastern Europeans possessed *yiddische herzen* (Jewish hearts)."[100]

The European voters in the Cleveland Convention, mostly immigrants, believed in this distinction, as did some of the American delegates. For the Pinsk crowd, the Cleveland Conference gave them a sense of empowerment and an arena to express their frustration with American Jewry and the culture that it had embraced. As the leader of the movement, Weizmann typified and reinforced the idea that European Jewry, especially from the East, represented the Jewish, *yiddishe*, Zionism that was genuine. Once the vote was taken and Weizmann the clear winner, Brandeis and his camp left defeated.

Although political Zionism was on the brink of collapse, the Cleveland Convention would boast a leader – albeit a minor figure in American Jewish politics – that would hopefully rejuvenate the movement. Born in Europe and at the time a local community rabbi in Kansas City, Rabbi Simon Glazer shared most of the views of Weizmann's political visions of Zionism, which led to a mutual bond between the two. At the conference, a meeting between Weizmann and Glazer would greatly impact the Zionist movement in the years to come.[101]

In recounting the history of the meeting in some of his personal letters, Glazer wrote that Weizmann informed him of "all the facts as they existed" about those who were protagonists or antagonists of Zionism.[102] Glazer then noted that the most important component of their conversation was when Weizmann told him what was needed to secure the success of Zionism:

> When he told me that if America would express in some manner its official sanction to the establishment of a Jewish national homeland in Palestine the doors of Palestine would be opened and every objection on the part of every nation would be removed, I thereupon determined that such an expression should be given by America, or I would know a reason why no such expression can be given. Dr. Weizmann accordingly commissioned me to do the work.[103]

Glazer accepted the task. However, that Weizmann would not only authorize but charge a local rabbi from a small Midwestern city to undertake a task that appeared so crucial to the Zionist movement's mission needs elaboration. Who was Simon Glazer? What convinced Weizmann that a small town rabbi could lobby the Congress and the White House to support Zionism? Would not it have been more prudent for Weizmann to have commissioned the Jewish power players in Washington? Surely they would have been in a much stronger position to open political doors than Glazer. And what of Brandeis and his camp? Naturally he felt affronted by the Weizmann debacle; yet he remained a strong Zionist. Would Brandeis not have agreed that a task so delicate – that of convincing the United States government that Zionism was in their best interest – that sending in a small town Orthodox rabbi to Washington may be counterproductive to the Zionist cause?[104] Regardless, Weizmann was convinced. Thereupon Glazer began the arduous task of lobbying on behalf of Zionism.

The Origin Of Glazer's Zionism

Rabbi Glazer's background made him an ideal choice for Weizmann. Precisely because of his lack of experience of Washington politics and because of his all-inclusive approach to Jews and Judaism, Glazer was an excellent choice to lobby on behalf of Zionism. His life experiences, especially as a youth, greatly affected his worldview, which eventually led to his involvement in Zionist politics. As a native of Eastern Europe, Glazer was first exposed to the Torah world of Lithuania, where he attended *yeshiva* (school of higher learning) until his eighteenth year, culminating in his obtaining rabbinical ordination. Shortly after he immediately moved to Tourvorig, a town near the Prussian border, to teach Torah to the synagogue and town members. Several months later, however, he was forced to leave. The Czar's Canton system that Jews so dreaded demanded that Glazer immediately join the Russian army. The Cantonist system (meaning "juvenile conscripts") was developed to break a boy's Jewish connection to Judaism – and boys like Glazer were a prime candidate – and supplant it with Russian mores. Military service, coupled with the ideals of Russian education and culture, devastated many Jewish communities. Consequently, Jews were forbidden to speak Yiddish while in the Cantonists. They were also forced to have lessons in Christianity. The Cantonist system, like tens of thousands of other Jewish families, greatly affected Glazer's worldview, which most likely played a significant role in his support for the creation of a Jewish national home.[105] After a short stint in the city of Koenigsberg, he left for Palestine in 1896. Unlike his experience in the aforementioned cities, however, Glazer was prompted to leave Palestine in 1897, as there was no work for him.[106]

Although disheartened that he could not stay in the Holy Land, yet proud of the Jews there, Glazer arrived in New York.[107] By 1902 he had married and taken several positions as a teacher. He learned English, studied secular sciences and to the best of his ability taught himself the histories of the world's civilizations. He also studied American law. Although he did not attend law school, or legally practice law in the United States, he considered himself to be somewhat of a lay expert in many areas of American civil discourse.[108] By the end of 1902, Glazer moved to Des Moines, Iowa, where he became the rabbi of the B'nai Israel Congregation. In Des Moines (and Sioux City), Glazer witnessed a controversial episode that left a lasting impression on him and the Jewish community.

Prior to Glazer's arrival, several Jewish women were instrumental in raising the needed funds to build a Reform temple (1898). Following the dedication of the synagogue the community had grown to several hundred. According to Glazer, "It (the Reform) has invaded every prosperous Jewish house in that city" (Des Moines).[109] He points out that, ironically (and it appears that he is being facetious) the Reform congregation, Mt. Sinai, changed the day of worship from Saturday to Sunday. This may appear to be radical, he writes, but even more disturbing is that Congregation Mt. Sinai, intentionally, "does not shelter a single *Sefer Torah* (a Torah scroll*)*."[110] Comically, Glazer writes, that "Strange, indeed, that the Law of Moses should be banished from Mt. Sinai."[111]

Glazer only spent three years in Sioux City before moving to Toledo, Ohio in 1907, where he began serving the B'nai Israel Congregation for two years. In Toledo, Glazer's ability to speak English improved dramatically, and he achieved a fluency level almost comparable to many American rabbis.[112] He later took a more high profile position as rabbi in Montreal, Quebec, where he remained for eleven years. In Montreal, Glazer was exposed to an influential Jewish community that was also very political in many aspects. He played a key role in trying to unify the community. In the 1920s, the community looked to Glazer for guidance regarding fundraising and Zionist ambitions. Glazer became instrumental in securing kosher food for many of Montreal's observant Jews. He also taught laymen of the community important *kashrut* regulations as well as trained several communal members how to conduct a *Shabbat* (Sabbath) service. Aside from religious instruction, Glazer also strengthened Jewish education throughout the Montreal Jewish community. He organized a federation of Jewish charities, and helped in the establishment of the YMHA (Young Men's Hebrew Association).[113] Following his departure from Montreal, Glazer served several other cities in the United States, including Seattle, Washington.

While in Seattle from 1918-1920, Glazer was instrumental in sustaining a small, yet cohesive Orthodox community. Glazer was well received at Congregation Bikkur-Cholim-Machzikay Hadath, the most prominent Ashkenazik Orthodox synagogue in Washington State. Although the Seattle Jewish community was about to grow into a thriving population with the influx of many Sephardic Jews, Glazer departed before their arrival.[114] In 1920, Glazer moved to Kansas City,

Missouri, where he served the Jewish community for three years in all aspects of communal work.[115] During these years, Glazer was also an ardent advocate on behalf of Zionism.

After serving the Midwest for several years, he lived in New York City from 1923-1927, presiding over the Beit Midrash Hagadol in Harlem, and then to Brooklyn where he became the rabbi of Temple Beth-El from 1927-1930. He eventually ended his rabbinic career in Manhattan, returning to serve the Maimonides Synagogue for eight years until his death in 1938.

Aside from his religious and spiritual guidance, Glazer was also a participant in many Jewish organizations with differing agendas. He was an affiliate of numerous rabbinical associations and was a respected confidant of Zionist organizations, including the Zionist Organization of America and the Mizrahi. Some of his participation in the various Jewish organizations led to clashes with the more right-wing Haredi (often referred to as "Ultra-Orthodox") branch of the Knesset ha-Rabbonim, who opposed Glazer's support of Zionism, as well as his advocacy for Sunday school education for Jewish children. Regardless of the critiques, he defended and supported varying Jewish causes, both communal and non-communal.[116] When Glazer died in 1938, his influence and contributions were essentially forgotten by history.

Aside from the political aspirations, Glazer also strove for a cohesive and self-sustained Jewish community in Palestine. By 1920, the *Yishuv* was still in its infancy. Unemployment, medical facilities, clean water, and a host of other relevant services needed to be created and sustained. Many foreign Jewish organizations attempted to and succeeded in playing a pivotal role in the development of the *Yishuv*. One such organization was the Keren Hayesod, the Palestine Foundation Fund, which supported Jewish colonization and land purchase.

Glazer played an important role in raising needed funds for Keren Hayesod, especially throughout the 1920s. He had coordinated a fund raising program between Keren Hayesod and other Jewish organizations and individual Jews. Thus, for example, the Zionist Organization of America and individual synagogues such as the Harlem Beit Hamidrash Hagadol, under the auspices of Glazer, often combined forces to raise funds for the Palestine cause.

The Zionist Organization of America often sought Glazer's counsel. This is clearly demonstrated when Abraham Goldberg, Secretary of the Palestine Bureau, implored Glazer to create an organization that would help spread public awareness about the necessity of creating a Jewish national home in Palestine. The organization's goal was to reach out to the American (and British) Christian population, beseeching them to rally for the Jewish claim and right to Palestine. Several years later, Glazer and Goldberg would collaborate in the quest for American government support of Zionism.[117]

Glazer did, however, have his political headaches. He was often asked to raise funds for various projects aside from Zionist causes. Glazer also was caught between two Jewish groups who clashed on practical Zionism issues. For instance, he was taken to task for allowing the Kansas City Jewish community to help appoint as head of the community one who opposed the Keren Hayesod. As noted above, he also clashed with his colleagues in the Knesset ha-Rabbonim regarding his support for Zionism as well.

Glazer was also a confidant of Mizrahi, the Orthodox Zionist organization.[118] A popular lecturer and at times, a favorite speaker, he influenced large numbers of people. From various archival materials, one can clearly discern that Glazer was a dynamic public speaker, where audience members were sometimes captivated by his lectures.[119] The Mizrahi movement's main tenets and the overall religious Zionist view are as follows: The land of Israel for the people of Israel according to the Torah of Israel. Comprised of Orthodox rabbis who believed that Zionism was not only a solution to the problem of the Diaspora, Mizrahi believed it was the means to bring about the redemption of the Jewish people, something Glazer fully ascribed to.[120] Glazer also asserted that the redemption of the Jews was dependent upon the Jewish masses physically returning to reside in the land of Israel.[121] In the Holy Land, he said, the Jews could live out their destiny and "yield to the world once more the spiritual fruit which has, since the days of the prophets, made this world worth living in."[122]

On numerous occasions, however, Glazer publicly complained about various Jewish groups who denied the political process of Zionism, as well as the theological process of redemption. In fact, some of these Jewish groups had differing reasons why they did not support Jewish nationhood. From Glazer's point of view, there were two fundamental reasons for their disagreement of and opposition to Zionism. The first group asserted that the land of Israel is neither central nor part of God's plan for the People of Israel. These "pious Orthodox Jews," as Glazer referred to them, believed that only with the Messiah's arrival would they be allowed to return to the Holy Land.[123] They also stated that in order to be "a light unto the nations" the Jews needed to be living throughout the cities of the world. In Glazer's words:

> There is a philosophy among a remnant few amongst the
> Jewish people that the Jews should forever remain in the Diaspora
> as missionaries to deliver the message of God to all nations.[124]

Although Glazer refers to this group as "a remnant few amongst the Jewish people," he states that they are a powerful and influential group that has wreaked considerable damage upon the Zionist movement and has taken hostage some of Judaism's most sacred texts. This group included the Agudath Yisrael. Glazer believed that this group's opposition to Zionism would have to be rectified.[125]

The second group, also held in contempt by Glazer, was comprised of those Jews (who have incidentally been influenced by the first group) that believed that supporting Zionism was tantamount to dual loyalty. The dual loyalists, Glazer writes, were afraid that they will be viewed by the overall American population as traitors, and that eventually, because of their support of a Jewish homeland, would be treated like second-class citizens. This group, he asserts, was also afraid for their well being throughout American society and, on a more global scale, that world Jewry would be in danger of losing their respective citizenship as well.[126] Glazer denied both groups' assertions as either wrong or misguided.

What is striking about Glazer's Zionism is that he had to break free from his upbringing in Lithuania where the vast majority of the Jews had not initially embraced the Zionist movement. Even in the United States, Orthodox rabbis, both as individuals and as members of institutions, lashed out at secular Zionism. Some found great fault with Glazer for supporting the Zionist movement. Even though these rabbis recognized Glazer's distinction of secular and religious Zionism, he was still branded in some circles as a heretic.

Glazer's theological support of Zionism can be traced years prior to his arrival in Palestine. In fact, although he was raised in Lithuania in an almost cool reception or even hostile environment in regards to Zionism, he studied in yeshiva under an early supporter of the *Hibbat Zion* (or *Hovevei Zion - Lovers of Zion)*, the first significant political organization (early 1870s) of the modern era that strove for Jewish autonomy in the land of Israel. Rabbi Alexander Moses Lapidot and his *Beit Din* (Court of Law) ordained (*semicha*) Rabbi Glazer. Rabbi Lapidot was an advocate of the Hovevei Zion and later joined the ranks when it was founded in Russia (1881). He advocated taking back the land of Israel, not through military conquest, but through agricultural labor that was rooted in religious doctrine. It should be assumed that Glazer's "Rebbe" (his spiritual rabbinic mentor) influenced him in respect to his eventual outlook regarding Zionism and the creation of a Jewish homeland in *Eretz Yisrael*.[127] This spiritual Zionism would eventually lead Glazer to a practical approach to acquire the land of Israel. Coupled with the positive teachings of his schooling as a young man, as well as his negative life experiences that ranged from the dreaded Cantonists to being forced to leave Palestine because no work existed, to various kosher problems throughout his travels in North America, all convinced Glazer that a Jewish national home was mandatory. After all, with a cohesive and self-sustaining Jewish homeland, the negative effects of the Diaspora would be made null and void for future generations. Simply put the Jews would be in charge of their own fate. Glazer did not have the opportunity to facilitate or be part of such a vision, at least on a "large" scale, until Weizmann approached him for help with lobbying. Once Weizmann asked Glazer to assist in the Zionist campaign, he immediately began the task.

Practical Zionism

Since Glazer was shortly to commence his lobbying initiatives both at the local and national level, he had to be fluent in the practical accomplishments of Zionism. Essentially, Glazer would need to show that Zionism was sustainable. A concern within the movement was stagnation, or worse, regression. Without the growth of what was known as "Practical Zionism" it was doubtful that the United States or other world powers would lend support for the establishment of a Jewish state. For if the Jews could not maintain a state, particularly long-term, there would be little reason to support its creation.

Practical Zionism began to take force during and subsequent to the Second *Aliyah* (immigration of Jews – 1903-1914) to Palestine. It was a movement that built its foundation on the roots of immigration of the Jewish masses. Once Jews were to arrive in Palestine, the settlers were to inhabit or create rural settlements with the intention of creating viable Jewish townships. To make a deserted parcel of land flourish, agricultural education and other technological knowledge such as water irrigation and soil cultivation was mandatory. Therefore, Practical Zionism also advocated the need for education. Ideally, such education would be centered in a university.[128] In 1925, Hadassah, the largest women's Jewish organization in the world (still today), had taken pride that they were an instrumental player in the creation of the Hebrew University of Jerusalem. However, no Jewish university in Palestine existed when Glazer began his lobbying.

Practical Zionism also entailed the development of hospitals where research and development could commence. With so many Jews becoming infected in the malaria infested swamps of Palestine, Henrietta Szold, the founder of Hadassah, lamented over the inhospitable situation of the land that had caused scores of deaths. Incidentally, many severely sick *halutzim* (pioneers) approached the heads of settlements begging for admission to hospitals that did not yet exist. Szold, acutely aware of the situation, and distraught over the medical conditions, attempted to create a main hospital hub, which was eventually located in Jerusalem.[129] While areas such as education and medical care were given significant attention, there were other Practical Zionist issues that were also important. One such example was business investment, which was also considered crucial to the development of the *Yishuv*.[130]

It should be emphasized that the noted components were to be created and implemented *without* Jewish political autonomy. Although some Jews would be allowed to administer aspects of the *Yishuv*, the Ottomans hampered Jewish immigration and the British later followed this policy.[131] Without able bodies, it would be close to impossible for the Jews to set up a state. Therefore, many Jewish groups had dedicated significant resources to bring Jews to Palestine. Money, for instance, was not just allocated to purchase boat tickets and the like, but was used to lobby governments, and even bribe officials for additional immigration visas and land purchases.

Many Zionists believed that with sufficient Jewish bodies living in and building up Palestine, a Jewish state would be inevitable.[132] Glazer, at the same time, both accepted and rejected this notion. Although Jewish bodies were mandated if the Jews were to be a majority of Palestine's population, he alleged that a secular people – which was the majority of Palestine's Jewish population – would never succeed. It would simply lack the basic structures needed to survive, the most important being the Law of Moses.[133] Repeatedly, Glazer reiterated his misgivings about those Jews who believed they could succeed in creating a viable country without God in the equation.

> How can a people (Israel), entirely devoted to things spiritual, diverge itself from its past and create a purely materialistic foundation for its future?[134]

Even though Glazer had great admiration for the *halutzim*, he still took them to task for their violations of Judaism. These secular, irreligious beliefs, (Glazer refers to them as "haughtiness") were a product of the *Galut*, the Exile of the Jewish people. As a reaction to *Galut*, Glazer writes, the Jews had reached hasty conclusions, and many came to believe that Judaism was irrelevant to achieve one's goals. Precisely because many Jews no longer felt the need to observe the Torah, while steadfastly holding onto the idea that Jews constituted a nation, migrating to Palestine seemed to be the right decision.[135] Glazer offers an explanation why many Jews, both religious and non-religious, felt the need to help in the creation of a Jewish homeland, using England as an illustration. (Incidentally, he would offer similar rationales in his dialogue with various government officials over the next two years while lobbying support for Zionism.)

For some reason, during the ruling years of the late Chief Rabbi

Herman Adler (1872-1946), the question of the legality of a Jewish divorce in England took the Jewish community by surprise. The House of Commons, the sole body in charge of the *"Get* Inquiry" proceedings, appointed a Royal Commission. Apparently, many Anglican Christian officials felt that a Jewish divorce within English borders was simply illegal, despite the fact that Jews had been living, and divorcing, in England for several hundred years by this point. A hearing was held where the Jews argued their case. When the verdict was delivered, however, many rabbis and Jewish leaders felt that it might become virtually impossible to issue a Jewish divorce in Great Britain, as new laws were to be created that would hinder the power of the rabbinic institutions.[136] This episode left a lasting and dark impression on Glazer. Consequently, this episode only reinforced Glazer's notion that the only solution to such double standards would be for Jews to have their own home. Even though this episode preoccupied British Jewry, for Glazer, it pertained to the entire Jewish people. He argued that this was not the first time such travesty and hypocrisy occurred against the Jews and that it would not be the last. The Jews had suffered in almost all countries where they lived and countless such duplicitous incidents had threatened the very fabric of Jewish life. He lashed out at non-Jewish governments' inimical attitude to Jews.

> Where there was no alternative they (Jews) suffered tyrannical laws and iniquity. The Jews, in their prayers, bless God for having "chosen them from among all peoples and exalted them above all nations;" therefore, they cannot be humbled and reduced to the grade of an inferior people which requires a special brand of government in order to subdue them.[137]

Glazer believed that with the creation of a Jewish national home such acts against the Jews would cease. However, it was not just these anti-Jewish edicts that perturbed Glazer, but acts of violence and terror were also high on his agenda.

In his writings on the Balfour Declaration, Glazer listed several examples of terror and murder against the Jews that had been commonplace since the dawn of the Jewish exile, such as expulsions and murder. In Russia, for example, he points out that the May Laws of 1881, which imposed massive restrictions on where Jews could physically live, led to both comprehensive expulsions and ruthless pogroms.[138] While Russia was busy persecuting their Jews, Germany, too, was trying to cover up its own problems by scapegoating them for the country's problems. For Glazer, this "barbaric treatment" demonstrated that "the Jewish people are one national unit" and should be considered as such by the nations of the world, especially those who mistreat the Jews.[139] His personal experiences and his solidarity with world Jewry led Glazer to accept Weizmann's proposition without hesitation.

Still, Glazer had yet to begin his campaign to convince the US Congress and President that a Jewish national home was an important endeavor worthy of their support. This was to be pursued on all levels of the political arena, from state assemblies to the White House. Much of this lobbying would take many months to bear fruit, but for Glazer the struggle for the hearts and souls of Christian Americans would be a battle well worth waging.

Politics

For several years after the issuance of the Balfour Declaration in November 1917, many supporters of Zionism hoped for a similar American pronouncement. Following the splitting of the Zionist movement at the Cleveland Conference of June 1921, Weizmann, as noted, believed that with American government affirmation of Zionism, Jewish statehood would shortly transpire. Over the course of five years, from 1917-1922, Glazer would play a pivotal role in this endeavor, firstly on his own volition, and later, after Cleveland, at the behest of Weizmann and the Zionist movement.

During his tenor as the head of Kansas City Jewry, aside from his daily activities within the community, Glazer petitioned the citizens of the State of Missouri to endorse the ideals of Zionism. His many contacts throughout the American South and Midwest that date from the time when he was the leading rabbi in Missouri later became his political allies, especially when he needed doors opened in Washington. Several Midwest government officials whom Glazer befriended in his early days in Kansas City later rose to more prominent positions (for instance from governor to senator to vice president). His early acquaintances would later bear fruit when the issue of American support for Zionism came to a vote in Congress.

Following the proclamation of the Balfour Declaration, a wave of enthusiasm engulfed large segments of world Jewry. Many Jews were overjoyed that after so many centuries of persecution and wandering, they were finally to have a home again of their own. Shortly after the declaration, Zionist groups mobilized their forces in an attempt to persuade Great Britain to implement its promise. However, even though England affirmed their support for a Jewish homeland in Palestine, many in the government were duplicitous when dealing with the Jews. Many Jewish groups and individuals, including Glazer, were skeptical of England's word.[140] Nevertheless, he reasoned that the same societal ideals that helped England create the Balfour Declaration could be used in the United States to sway members of the government to support Zionism.

Glazer believed that the outpouring of support by the Jews regarding Palestine as their future homeland influenced Britain to create such a petition.

British statesmen could not ignore a movement which received publicity in every civilized country. The very nature of the Diaspora made the movement universally known, and therefore respected in every chancellery.[141]

As Glazer notes, an additional component that led to the Balfour Declaration was the fact that for centuries, England wrongly considered British Jewry "separate" from the rest of world Jewry. This view later changed, however. One of the highest priorities of Zionist organizations in the battle for support was to convince the average Englishman that the Jews constituted an indivisible nation that had been separated geographically for centuries. This approach, he believed, may have convinced the British that the Jewish people are in fact one national unit.[142]

Aside from the attempt to convince the average Brit that the Jews were a national unit (just in exile), other important initiatives, equally if not more important than the previous discussion, would also have to be undertaken and achieved. Firstly, Glazer believed that a media campaign was necessary to show the average Englishman that a Jewish homeland in Palestine was a necessity. Placed in newspapers, magazines and other avenues of communication, this media campaign would be ever important for the Jewish people. If, on a daily scale, Great Britain could be convinced that supporting a Jewish national home in Palestine was in the best interest of the Empire, Jewish groups believed they could achieve their goal.[143]

Another tactic – perhaps the greatest – that was used to convince England that a Jewish national home was important was the invocation of the Bible. By utilizing Biblical sources in the Old and New Testaments to prove that the land of Israel rightfully belonged to the Jews, Jewish groups were playing a dangerous, yet important game.[144] Glazer believed that "The Britishers are a Biblical people." They read the Bible daily, attempt to internalize its message, and live by its dictates. Furthermore, the British were the first to translate the Bible into English (which Glazer liked to point out in more than one place). Even though he believed that the announcement of the Balfour Declaration was a political maneuver, Glazer believed that a more important aspect of the decision to create the proclamation was because of the Bible.[145]

In fact, Glazer writes when Arthur Balfour (the author of the Balfour Declaration) came to the United States and Canada in 1916, the first person to speak with him about Palestine was Clarence I. Desola, the Jewish Consul General of Belgium stationed in Montreal, Quebec. In Montreal, Desola gave his opinion to Lord Balfour regarding the Jews' claim to Palestine, and invoked Biblical references to strengthen his assertions. During the conversation, Balfour told Desola (the first Jew according to Glazer to hear such a pronouncement) that Great Britain would soon issue a proclamation calling for an eventual Jewish national home in Palestine.[146] As for the Biblical references stated in their conversation, Glazer gives somewhat of an overview. Subsequently, he repeatedly invoked such references with American government officials when discussing Zionism.

Glazer notes that after many centuries, Great Britain had finally gained a "foothold in the Holy of Holies", the land of Israel. If the decision to implement the Balfour Declaration is undertaken, he reasoned, Britain will "mete out historic justice to the people which made it the Holy of Holies," the Jews.[147] Following the publicizing of the Balfour Declaration, many spoke in terms "that historic justice *has been* meted out." Glazer reasoned that with the recognition that Palestine, or at least parts of it belong to the Jews – an idea suppressed by the Catholic Church and Christianity in general for centuries because of the Jewish rejection of Jesus – Great Britain showed a great form of evenhandedness and integrity towards the Jewish people, and to world history.[148]

Even though England made such a proclamation, other countries and powerful city-states rejected it. Glazer writes that France rejected the claim for political reasons while the Vatican rejected it on theological grounds. France's objections, however, were more numerous than the Vatican's. The French claimed that too few Jews resided in Palestine, and therefore no state was deserved. An example that France reiterated on more than one occasion was that the Palestinian imbroglio did not resemble post World War I countries such as Poland and other Eastern and Central European states. Created with greater land following the war, Poland's population reached many millions. This was also true for Latvia, Lithuania, Courtland, Finland, and the Slovak countries. The issue of Palestine "was most perplexing," not only to the French, Glazer wrote, but to other "statesmen of many chancelleries, including the United States State Department."[149] More will be said later regarding the French, Vatican and the Department of State's positions regarding Zionism during the opposition phase of the Palestine Lodge Resolution of 1922.

The underlying theme of Glazer's discourse was to highlight the most important ingredients when dealing with non-Jewish authorities. These included arguments such as the Bible is proof that the land of Israel belongs to the Jews, and if Palestine becomes a Jewish homeland, justice will finally be obtained. These two arguments would be used in countries where Jews tried to garner support for Zionism. Additionally, such talking points would be quite relevant when dealing with American government officials.[150] Even though Glazer believed that these subjects were significant and were valued by non-Jews, many in the Zionist movement feared that the Balfour Declaration would be challenged and quite possibly marginalized, or at the very worst forgotten.

A significant reason why Zionist leaders harbored these sentiments stemmed from the reaction of the Arab world following the Balfour Declaration. Arab states, and those aspiring for independence in the Middle East, vehemently opposed any action that would alter the status quo of Palestine. It may well be that Arab leaders preferred Christian control over Palestine to that of Jewish rule, however.[151] In any event, not only did Arab rulers send envoys to Europe in the attempt to garner support for the reversal of the Balfour Declaration, but as will be shown later, representatives from the Arab world attempted to lobby American leaders across the political spectrum to resist the push for American support of any future resolution favoring the Jews' claim to Palestine.

Well aware that a campaign such as the Arab federations were mounting would eventually turn into an anti-Semitic springboard and age-old stereotypes would be used to debunk the Jews and their claim to Palestine, Jewish groups began preparing counter-offensives to offset Arab claims. In one major incident, Glazer singlehandedly opposed a Syrian delegation that had traveled to the southern states of America who attempted to sway the political leaders – both governors and senators – that Zionism is criminal and that the Jews are evil. Within three hours of being informed that the Syrian delegation was spreading lies about the Palestinian Jewish community and the Jewish people as a whole, Glazer set his own agenda.

The Syrian delegation had arrived in Topeka, Kansas, Glazer's Jewish community, sometime before September 19, 1921 with the intention of meeting with Governor Henry J. Allen. They intended, Glazer notes, to dissuade the Governor from supporting Zionism. Deciding that they must be stopped, Glazer immediately sent word to his colleagues that the Syrian delegation would be prevented from appearing in Jefferson City (where the Governor resided) if he had any say.

By this time, Glazer had been intimate with Governor Allen for over fifteen years. That same night he sent a special message to Allen's residence. In his own words, Glazer writes that the governor "would have to meet me at 11:30 next morning."[152] The following morning when Glazer arrived at the Governor's mansion, Allen told him what the Syrian delegation hoped to achieve. In short, the Governor noted that the delegation's goal was to prevent the Jews from creating a home in Palestine as long as the Arabs, and the Syrians in particular, were in the region.

Glazer requested that Governor Allen refuse to meet with the Syrian delegation. He relates that Allen immediately approved of such a move, and from that moment on, the Syrian delegation never met the Governor. Furthermore, Glazer writes that Allen would then contact various governors from the Southwest, the Midwest, and the Pacific Coast imploring them not to meet with the Syrian delegation as well. All state governors complied, Glazer notes, with Governor Allen's request.[153] The following week the Syrian delegation left the United States and made the long and disappointed journey back to Syria.[154]

After he had successfully convinced Allen not to meet with the Syrian delegation, who in turn lobbied his colleagues across the American South and West to do the same, Glazer proceeded to create public awareness of the Zionist campaign. As the English Jewish community had done, Glazer attempted to utilize newspapers and other avenues of communication that would help popularize and bring the ideals of Zionism to the Christian masses. His first task was to convene a conference of Jewish representatives of the states of Iowa, Nebraska, Kansas, Missouri and Oklahoma, with the hopeful outcome that each state would work with the other to garner support for Zionism. The "Kansas City Conference of Jewish Representative," as it came to be known, accomplished many of their goals.[155]

The Conference was not only successful in promoting Zionism, though, but was also an avenue and means to combat anti-Semitism. Several collaborating plans were implemented by the Conference. Although somewhat effective in garnishing support for Zionism, as well as combating anti-Semitism, without Glazer, the Conference would have achieved little. In fact, Glazer was successful in the Southwestern states precisely because he worked with many different Jewish groups, where he often brought varying agendas together. For instance, the Zionist Organization of America (ZOA) often called upon Glazer to intervene with prominent non-Jewish officials in the South on behalf of Zionism.

In one major development, the ZOA, in a panic mode, wrote to Glazer imploring him to intervene with his local and state newspapers. Apparently, the ZOA feared that attacks on Zionism could tarnish the movement.

> Our opponents are gathering anew their forces to combat Zionism. They are using every means of propaganda to defeat our purpose, and to secure the annulment of the Balfour Declaration. This insidious propaganda must be counteracted, and counteracted effectively.[156]

During this episode, the ZOA sent Glazer information that had been created solely for counteracting the claims against Zionism. In turn, Glazer would use his influence and network to have the information printed in the editorials of all the major newspapers of the State. In the words of the General Secretary of the ZOA, "The public must be properly informed on all matters relating to the Jewish Homeland, and public opinion... should be placed on record."[157] Glazer was told to "make this your personal business" and to feel personally that it was he who was being attacked. After Glazer had secured support from his local and state newspapers to print the information, he was "to report to the ZOA immediately."[158]

In fact, the ZOA utilized Glazer's talents and connections many times. One week prior to the General Secretary of the ZOA's letter to Glazer, he had received a letter from Abraham Goldberg, Secretary of the Palestine Bureau, who also sat on the Administrative Committee. He had a special proposal for Glazer, one that he believed only the rabbi could accomplish. Goldberg had written Glazer in reaction to Alfred Northcliffe, one of the largest magazines and newspapers distributors in England and a rabid anti-Semite. During this time, Northcliffe was attempting to organize support for the rescinding of the Balfour Declaration.[159] Similar to what transpired in Italy and Switzerland, Goldberg noted, the American Jewish community (under Glazer's leadership) should attempt to create "a society of gentiles." By utilizing Christian support for the eventual creation of a Jewish country they could also be an important instrument to offset the negative sentiments in the United States that people like Northcliffe propagated in England.[160]

The "society of gentiles" would be called either the "Pro-Jewish-Palestine" society, or a more abridged name like "Pro-Judaea." Membership in the "Pro-Judaea" was to consist of the most prominent public and private gentile officials, including politicians, businessmen, and clergy. Furthermore, Goldberg writes, "very few Jews participating" is also a necessity. The society would support Zionism "to the best of their ability," and would help lobby powerful politicians who could assist in securing financial resources for the creation of the Jewish homeland.[161] Also, ironically, the society was to engage in prayer for the success of Zionism as well.[162] According to Goldberg, only with such an organization can the Zionists "counter-act all these calumnies, in England, as well as in this country (United State)." Whether or not Glazer successfully accomplished and implemented the "Pro-Judaea," the attempt demonstrates that he was looked upon as someone who could accomplish what many Jewish leaders could not. In the United State a pro-Zionist campaign (similar to what transpired in England) deserved the full attention of the American Jewish community to counteract the negative propaganda that was being spread by the enemies of the Jews.[163]

By July 1921, Glazer had personally written numerous articles in several newspapers published throughout Kansas and Missouri. The ZOA notes that many of his articles were welcomed across the political and religious spectrums of the southern states, and by Zionist organizations in New York.[164] Louis Lipsky, the Secretary General of the ZOA, felt compelled to express his gratitude to Glazer for "his excellent articles" and promised him all the support he needed to continue his campaign. Shortly thereafter, Glazer received letters from powerful politicians such as senators and governors, promising Glazer that Arab delegations bent on the destruction of Zionism would not be tolerated in the United States.

Senator Charles Curtis, a prominent Senate leader and in charge of the Senate Floor, sent Glazer a letter in early September 1921 at the request of Governor Allen of Kansas, promising him assistance with Zionism and the opposing generalized "mayhem," such as what the Syrian delegation attempted to undertake. Curtis also promised Glazer that he would speak with officials at the State Department about future visits from such delegations. Two weeks later, the Governor of Nebraska, Samuel R. McKelvie, summoned Glazer for a meeting. Sent by Governor Allen of Kansas, Glazer was well received by Governor

McKelvie in his residency. Earlier, on the intervention and request of Allen, McKelvie was one of the governors who refused to meet with the Syrian delegation. Being familiar with some of McKelvie's accomplishments in Nebraska, Glazer was more than excited to meet with him.[165]

Glazer believed that McKelvie was one of the few politicians "who could put two and two together," meaning he would not be easily influenced by propagandists like the Syrians. Upon entering his chambers, McKelvie immediately began to question Glazer:

> Doctor Glazer, you stopped the Syrians. I am glad you came. Sit down, and tell me what it is all about.[166]

In a rather lengthy discourse Glazer began to explain the goals of Zionism. The mission and result of Zionism, he explained to McKelvie, was a secure homeland for the Jewish people. For too many centuries, he continued, the Jews had been living in "others" lands. Persecution, intolerance, expulsion, and murder at the hands of non-Jewish governments had been far too often the normative of the Diaspora.[167] The Jews only ask for a fair chance to create their own destiny. With good people and support from powerful individuals "such as yourself (Governor McKelvie) and Governor Allen," the Jews believe that their case will be made stronger. The result, he concluded, would be a Jewish homeland in Palestine.

Interrupting Glazer in the middle of his sermon, McKelvie proceeded to ask Glazer what type of cigarette he smoked, whereupon McKelvie gave him one. Before McKelvie spoke again, he had smoked several cigarettes and then proceeded to speak to Glazer:

> If the State of Nebraska cannot hold all the Jews that there are in the world, its citizens are certainly ready to do everything in their power to give Palestine for the rest of those that cannot be residents here.[168]

At the close of the meeting, Glazer felt assured that he had secured the good Governor's support for the cause of Zionism. Over time, Governor McKelvie intervened with powerful figures in the United States government, encouraging many of them to support Zionism.[169]

During the same year that Glazer lobbied governors from the Midwest and South to support Zionism, he actively raised funds for a variety of endeavors in Palestine. As his reputation spread and the more he became known as someone who could be relied on, Glazer was approached to raise needed funds for Zionist activity. On May 30, 1921 (a month before the Cleveland Conference), Glazer received a telegram from Louis Lipsky at the ZOA. The telegram was written in a vague, aggressive and almost desperate tone, asking Glazer to raise money for a yearly membership fee for the ZOA, from fifty individuals. The money would be placed in the ZOA bank account in New York City, and a portion of the funds would be used to pay for Glazer's trip to New York to meet with the leadership of the ZOA in an attempt to strategically plan their next moves.[170]

On the agenda in New York would be the percentage of funds that would be sent to the Keren Hayesod, the Palestine Foundation Fund, which by this time had for some years been buying land in Palestine on behalf of world Jewry. Keren Hayesod had been a favorite organization of the ZOA, and considered the organization essential to the movement's ultimate success.[171] Glazer too recognized the need and importance of Keren Hayesod. Throughout the southern states, Glazer was later asked to raise additional funds, under the auspices of the ZOA, which were to be transferred to Keren Hayesod.[172] In fact, throughout the year 1921, in addition to his lobbying activities, Glazer raised significant money for the fund.[173] His fundraising on behalf of Keren Hayesod, however, would not cease for many years.[174]

During the second half of 1921 Glazer's political career accelerated. He was called upon to help during the last moments of fundraising campaigns, or in an emergency. Weizmann, well of aware of Glazer's talents, had insisted that he personally see to it that the American government officially declare its support for Zionism. Glazer was now ready to enter a new political arena in an entirely different location. Glazer was about to enter the political life of Washington, D.C.

The Lobbying Of Government Officials

Following the British Balfour Declaration in 1917 Jewish and Zionist groups hoped for a similar American proclamation. To convince key politicians to support such a resolution, though, was no easy task. There were Jewish allies throughout the government, most importantly members of Congress that had aided the Jewish community over the years. Whether it would be possible to convince a majority of the Congress to support Zionist goals, however, or support the initial stance of the Balfour Declaration, was unclear. Even though Glazer was somewhat skeptical of securing Congressional support, nonetheless, he believed that such an endeavor would eventually succeed. Optimism permeated many in the Zionist movement and eventually Glazer was convinced that the Senate might pass such a resolution.

Initially, Glazer lamented over the "almost impossible" task that he was to undertake. The US government was so massive and with varying forces influencing policy, particularly after World War I, left Glazer unsure of the outcome. In fact, had he failed to secure American support for Zionism, he feared that such a setback would be counterproductive to the cause. What if, Glazer reasoned, he tried to persuade government officials and it backfired? Would they then perhaps fight against the goals of Zionism?[175] In any event, Weizmann and the Zionist Organization of America (ZOA) had convinced him to undertake the task.

From the inception of the Balfour Declaration and the initial lobbying of American officials, Glazer received both positive and negative messages from across the political spectrum. There was no clear agenda regarding Zionism within the entirety of the American government, which only irritated Glazer. At certain times immediately following his meetings, a sense of annoyance or jubilation could overtake him. Describing his experience fighting for the resolution, he wrote that "What a world of intrigue, tragedy, misleading propaganda, slander, despair, hard work and final triumph!"[176] Glazer often compared his lobbying initiatives and the pitfalls that came with it to that of English Jewry's experience leading up to – and immediately after – the issuance of the Balfour Declaration, where a climate of skepticism and frustration was most prevalent. Glazer's initial reaction to the frenzy surrounding the Balfour Declaration was one of uncertainty. Although he had initially believed that many British politicians were honest and straightforward, he later found many were not. Some had ill sentiments of Jews and would fight to ensure that a Jewish national home was never created.[177] Glazer feared that some in the United States would follow a similar example as the British.

No clearer was this fear manifested, Glazer noted, than when an anti-Semitic campaign ensued following the Balfour Declaration, where Jew-hatred escalated across Europe. According to Glazer, this was the worst anti-Semitism that the Jewish people had ever been exposed to.[178] Classical anti-Semitism such as leveling the charges of deicide (the Jews killed God) was a common slander. Since the Jews had killed Jesus, Church doctrine stated, they, like Cain (who killed his brother Abel), are condemned to wander the earth forever. Hence, they should never again be allowed to return to the Holy Land.[179] Religious and political anti-Semitism reached and eventually permeated the Arab world, which, as noted earlier, refused to accept the notion of a Jewish homeland in Palestine.[180] The Arab and Mohammedan world, "kinfolk of the Jewish people," Glazer writes, began fearing the Jews.

This anxiety climaxed in Jerusalem where, in 1920, "two Czar-like" pogroms against the Jews transpired.[181] Glazer explains that the propaganda was so severe in Palestine that Jews became "like rats in the eyes of the Arabs."[182] This manifestation of violent anti-Semitism deeply impacted in the *Yishuv*.

> The effect of the anti-Semitic propaganda was of such a depressing character that even the most hopeful Jewish patriots found themselves unable to cope with the situation. The new brand of propaganda against the Jewish people was sampled even here in our own country (US) – Mr. Henry Ford's brand for example.[183]

Even though virulent anti-Semitism was spreading in parts of the world, including the US, Glazer believed that it would have little, if any, effect upon the decisions of American government officials regarding Zionism. Consequently, he also believed that it would have little impact on Jewish migration to Palestine.[184]

When Glazer was selected by Weizmann to lead the campaign to convince the US government to support a pro-Zionist position and eventual resolution, and once he tasted Washington politics, he decided to create a team to assist. His initial team consisted of friends and colleagues that he had previously worked with, such as H. Conheim, Treasurer of Keren Hayesod (Palestine Foundation Fund), Abraham Goldberg, Secretary of the Palestine Bureau (and member of the Administrative Committee of the ZOA) and Louis Lipsky, General Secretary of the Zionist Organization of America. Glazer asked them to help create and implement a plan, and see to it that it was maintained.

Two months later in August, Glazer went to Washington in an attempt to discover the position of Congress on the Palestine issue, meeting with various government officials. Before long, however, Glazer was told by the State Department that such a resolution by Congress would likely never pass. Furthermore, friends in the State Department informed him that they personally disapproved of such a resolution on the grounds that "it might be wrongly interpreted by some foreign powers and breed complication."[185] Even though Glazer explicitly stated that the State Department harbors some bias towards the Jewish people, he implied that "prejudice or bigotry has yet reached... our real leaders."[186]

Following Glazer's disappointed meeting with officials from the Department of State, he decided that he would have to contact leading statesmen who had confidence in the present administration. He then headed back to the Midwest. One week later, Glazer met with his old friend Governor Allen of Kansas. After a lengthy discussion, Glazer presented his entire action plan. After Glazer answered Allen's questions, the Governor responded that a resolution by Congress supporting a future homeland for the Jewish people would "without a doubt have the desired effect."[187] Glazer left reassured that Allen would do all in his power on behalf of Zionism.

Glazer conversation with Allen was reinforced by a letter that Glazer received from the Governor, explaining to him that a prominent Senate leader, Charles Curtis, found no fault in bringing such a resolution to the Senate Floor. The resolution would first have to be written and then approved by the State Department. If the State Department found fault with the resolution, Allen continued, it would have to be amended. Although few aside from the State Department was concerned about the minor details of the resolution, the State Department, Glazer was told, had to be meticulous and careful about what they endorsed.[188]

Governor Allen also explained in his letter to Glazer that he was encouraged that such a powerful leader as Senator Curtis sympathized with the Jewish people. Most significantly, Allen noted that Curtis would gladly assist Glazer in the formulation of the resolution and that he would help convince other senators that the resolution was important and that it should be passed.[189] In a letter dated September 13, 1921, one-week prior to Allen's letter to Glazer, Senator Curtis had written to Governor Allen explaining the politics regarding the intended Zionist resolution. In his letter, Curtis requested that Glazer send him a copy of the resolution (however, it had not been completed). Curtis would then review it and take the matter up with the State Department. The only reservation Curtis had regarding the resolution appears to be the very same reluctance of State Department officials, namely that "complications not arise."[190] Curtis ended his letter by saying that "Personally my sympathies are with the Jewish people, and I would like to see them establish a national home in Palestine."[191] When Glazer received the letter from Governor Allen informing him that Senator Curtis would do all he could for the cause of Zionism, he immediately praised Allen for his efforts.[192]

Shortly after, Glazer headed for Jefferson City, Missouri, to meet with Governor Hyde. Hyde had long been acquainted with Glazer and his work on behalf of the Kansas City Jewish community. Throughout the conversation with the Governor, Glazer writes, Hyde grasped all the details at hand and became a great supporter of the Zionist cause. Specifically, the Governor endorsed a Senate resolution supporting the creation of a Jewish national home in Palestine.

Immediately after their meeting, Governor Hyde wrote a letter to Sheldon P. Spencer, one of the two Senators of the state of Missouri, asking him to get involved in the matter. When informed that Hyde wrote Spencer, Glazer appeared ill at ease. Glazer had requested that such information be made known to the Governor only after he was more educated of the situation. After, he could then request that his state senators support Zionism. Nonetheless, Glazer was later pleased with Hyde's intervention. The Governor explained in a letter to Glazer that he believed he was informed enough to begin writing on behalf of Zionism.[193]

Senator Spencer's reply to Governor Hyde was not found in any searched archives, although Hyde quotes a portion of his response in a letter to Glazer. The letter Hyde wrote to Glazer seems to be full of enthusiasm, especially when he quotes Senator Spencer's reaction to his request. Spencer wrote the following:

> You are entirely right in what you state concerning my attitude in this matter. Anything I can do for that race I shall be

glad to do. I can never forget that my Savior was himself a Jew, and the suffering of this people in their years of wandering and persecution is tragic.[194]

Commenting on this letter, Glazer wrote that his confidence in "our own great western men were confirmed." His reservations with some individuals in the US government did not change his view that "great prejudice or bigotry has yet reached…. our real leaders."[195]

Continuing his tour, Glazer traveled to Nebraska, meeting with his old friend, Governor McKelvie. Glazer found McKelvie in high spirits, smoking a cigarette. He could tell by the look on his face, between puffs, that McKelvie and the people of Nebraska "know what they are doing."[196] On September 29, 1921, Governor McKelvie sent Glazer a letter along with a copy of a memo that he had sent to the two Senators of Nebraska, Gilbert M. Hitchcock and George W. Norris. In the letter to the Senators, McKelvie conveyed his sympathy and approval. He also said that he wanted the Senate to pass a resolution endorsing a Jewish homeland in Palestine. His simple reservation was that this task must "be in harmony and purposes of the Department of State of the United States."[197]

Senator Hitchcock, who at the time was the Minority Leader of the Senate, pledged his support for Zionism and reiterated that he would do all in his power to help the Jewish people. Glazer points out that Hitchcock's pledge referred to "practical issues." Governor McKelvie also vowed support for any measure that would help expedite the formation of a Jewish national home, including using his influence with a very close friend, Vice President Calvin Coolidge. Coolidge, Glazer writes, was also sympathetic to the Jewish people and, like Senator Hitchcock he was told, would work for practical solutions to "help carry out this noble ambition of the Jewish nation."[198] The noted individuals reasoned that a government resolution supporting the creation of a Jewish homeland was a necessary first step.

It was agreed that the initiative to bring the resolution to the Senate Floor would be spearheaded by Senator Charles Curtis. Curtis, as shown, pledged to review the resolution and then attempt to bring it to the Floor. By the end of September 1921, brushing aside any political obstacles, Senator Curtis agreed to take the cause under his wing.[199] Assured that Curtis would do all in his power to bring the resolution to a vote, Glazer then decided he had to convince the President of the United States to support such a resolution.

With the Zionist endeavor moving rather smoothly, Glazer felt compelled to write President Warren G. Harding. On the eve of *Rosh HaShanah,* the Jewish New Year, Glazer asked Harding to pray for the Jewish people, a nation whose "situation is bleak and unhappy."[200] He points out that with so many newly created states in Europe, Jews are still not part of any country. The British, he notes, had made a declaration proclaiming that a Jewish national home in Palestine be established. However, the creation of a Jewish national home will not materialize unless America, under the leadership of President Harding, gives its blessing. Glazer ended his letter to Harding stating that "the whole project will fail" if the President does not give his consent.[201] It is not clear if President Harding ever saw this letter.

Glazer and other Zionist figures such as Weizmann reasoned that the acquiescence of the American President was necessary because of the reservations voiced at the State Department (State). After months of negotiations with Glazer and other Zionist leaders, State was still incredulous to support the resolution.[202] Many officials at State seriously impeded Glazer's efforts, reinforcing the notion that some in the department refused to support Zionism when it came to trading territory of the former Ottoman Empire.[203]

In a letter dated October 17, 1921, Curtis wrote Glazer informing him that he had prepared a resolution supporting the creation of a Jewish homeland in Palestine. He took the draft to the State Department and was given the exact same answer that had been given to Glazer; that, at the present time, the affairs of the British Mandate of Palestine would not be considered until the Treaty of Peace between the Allies and Turkey were concluded.[204]

Glazer's frustration was mounting. On October 17, Glazer received another letter from Senator Curtis noting that there have been several setbacks. Although Curtis had been leading the mission in the Senate to pass a pro-Zionist resolution, and while the many delays irritated him, he still continued his efforts. He believed eventually that the State Department and the President would support the Zionist endeavor. Shortly after October 17, Curtis informed Glazer that he had taken the draft resolution to the State Department and was given the same response; that until peace between the Allies and Turkey was solidified, State would not support the resolution.[205]

After reading Curtis's letter, Glazer grew more disturbed. He was certain that officials of the State Department had already convinced themselves that a resolution supporting the creation of a Jewish homeland in Palestine was not going to pass unless more pressure was exerted on the Congress and White House.[206] He decided again to write Governor Allen to determine what course of action to follow. Allen replied (on October 21, 1921) that he was confident the resolution would eventually be submitted and passed, and promised Glazer that he could count on him whenever he needed help.[207] Although Allen did not suggest what his capabilities were to help the cause, Glazer was informed that the Disarmament Conference taking place in Europe in the aftermath of World War I had severely impinged his mission.

Glazer decided that something more aggressive needed to be undertaken. He believed that he had to draw the leading world powers, which had been negotiating a final truce in Europe, to seriously consider Zionism. In some fashion he had to place the Jewish and Zionist question directly before them. Only then, Glazer believed, did he stand a chance of succeeding. He decided that the most opportune time to act was when he was denied the ability to adopt five orphaned Jewish children from war torn Europe. Not only had these orphans witnessed World War I, but they all had been "victims of pogroms." The refusal to adopt the orphans left a lasting and dark impression on Glazer.[208] He decided that this was the appropriate time once again to visit Washington, and perhaps meet with the President.[209]

A Conversation With The President

Rabbi Glazer believed that the next necessary step to secure a proclamation by the United States in support of Zionism would be a successful meeting with the President, Warren G. Harding. The convincing of the President of the United States to back the creation of a Jewish national home in Palestine, Glazer reasoned, would be the greatest achievement in the Zionist process since the issuance of the Balfour Declaration. If Harding could be convinced, he alleged, all the pieces of the puzzle would come together. The State Department would have to accommodate the President's view, which in turn would lead the Senate to approve a proclamation in favor of a Jewish national home.

Prior to his attempt to meet with President Harding, Glazer had written Senator Curtis on November 10, 1921, imploring him to meet "sometime next week." The requested conference had two objectives: that Curtis arrange a meeting with the Chairman of Immigration in the Senate in order to discuss the situation of the five orphaned children that he had planned to adopt and to help set up an appointment to meet with President Harding.

After waiting several days for a reply, Glazer finally received a telegram from Curtis. The Senator said that he would first have to meet with Glazer and review the plan and then he could look into arranging a meeting with the President.[210] Hopefully the meeting would take place sometime in November 1921. As for Glazer's desired meeting with the Chairman of Immigration in the Senate, it was set for the following week.[211] Two days after receiving Curtis's telegram, another was sent to Glazer, happily informing him that "President Harding will see you Friday morning this week at ten thirty."[212]

Excited about his upcoming meeting with the President, Glazer wrote to the members of the Executive Committee of the World Zionist Organization (WZO) informing them that he would be meeting with Harding. He requested advice and guidance from the WZO, whereupon Henry J. Danenbaum and Abraham Goldberg were sent to meet Glazer in Washington. Both men had been highly influential in the WZO and had extensive contacts with numerous senators and politicians. Both, it was felt, would properly prep Glazer for the most important meeting of his political life and a critical one for Zionism.

While in Washington, the group created an action plan for Glazer's upcoming meeting with the President. A multitude of discussion points and questions (as well as responses) were drawn up, ranging from topics such as the Palestine resolution to combating anti-Semitism. As Glazer was examining a draft, Senator Curtis phoned his hotel and invited him to the Senate Chambers.

At the Senate Curtis explained to Glazer that it was impossible for him to introduce Glazer to Harding while the Senate was still in session. The introduction, he was told, would have to wait for a more opportune time. However, Curtis did give Glazer a letter of introduction (a major accomplishment), which ultimately was utilized in order to meet with the President. [213] The letter stated that President Harding would meet with Glazer on November 18, 1921 and that Harding should give Glazer a "fair meeting."

> This will introduce to you Rabbi Simon Glazer of Kansas City, Mo., to whom you agreed to give an interview at 10:30 Friday morning, November 18th. I take great pleasure in recommending the Rabbi to you and trust you will give him a full and complete hearing.
>
> (signed) Charles Curtis[214]

Glazer anxiously arrived at the White House early on November 18. At 10:35 a.m. he entered the Executive Office where he found President Harding seated. He was warmly received and was told that he had approximately thirty minutes to speak with the President. After a brief introduction Glazer wasted no time and began to discuss the present situation of European Jewry. He noted that during World War I and subsequent to the armistice, the Jewish population of Europe had been treated with wholesale contempt. Countless Jewish lives were lost and if the present situation was not remedied, more innocents would die. In ending the first part of their discussion, Rabbi Glazer remarked to President Harding: "Under your direction the prophecy of Isaiah, 'nation shall not lift sword against nation, nor shall they learn any more the art of war,' will be fulfilled."[215] Apparently, Glazer endeavored to create a feeling within Harding that he was God's emissary on Earth and that with his leadership, not only the Jews, but the entire world, would finally live in peace.

Convincing Harding that he was God's messenger was one of Glazer's most effective tactics during their discussion, and he could sense that his approach may work to his political advantage (this was not just rhetoric, as Glazer did believe Harding could be a harbinger of such times). Even though the Executive Branch, the State Department and a host of other agencies had been preoccupied with the Disarmament Conference, Zionists groups and Glazer believed that, with its conclusion, the United States would support a resolution calling for a Jewish national home. Glazer reiterated to Harding that he was leading the world to a time of harmony, where the "age old dream" of peace between neighbors would finally become apparent. Of course, this would not transpire until the Jews had a homeland of their own.[216]

From Harding's perspective, and therefore the White House's, the Disarmament Conference could have had a profound impact on Zionism. Had the Allies not secured an armistice agreement with Turkey, the Palestine imbroglio would not cease for years to come, nor would it be given any priority by England or the United States. Harding asked Glazer whether he intended to address the Disarmament Conference, even though Glazer had no plans to. Glazer, however, became defensive. His intentions were first to convince the American President that Zionism was important and in America's best interest. Only with the blessing of the United States, he reiterated, would other countries give their support to the Zionist endeavor. The President remarked, though, that Glazer could address the Conference with the intention of convincing the Allies, as well as its adversaries, that a Jewish national home in Palestine was the moral course of action.

Glazer feared that if he addressed the Conference he would create a climate of anti-Semitism, potentially permeating those states that had previously or currently had no relations with Jews or Zionism. Although he believed that he could acquire support from countries that were not anti-Semitic, he feared an intervention would be counterproductive. He told President Harding that

> There are nations represented at the Disarmament Conference who as of yet have not learned to be anti-Semitic and it would be dangerous to show them the way.[217]

Glazer also reasoned that to lobby various governments where a relationship with Jews was non-existent would prompt the Arabs to counteract.

The President appeared to agree with Glazer, but was confused – as well as intrigued – by one of his earlier comments. What led

Glazer to believe, Harding inquired, that the President of the United States could be instrumental in bringing about the actualization of Zionism, as well as become the "harbinger of peace in the world"? Glazer, well prepared to answer this question, explained that only the American President could convince England to implement the Balfour Declaration. Consequently, once this happens, it will usher in a time where Jewish independence would be achieved. Glazer surmised that not only would supporting Zionism be in the best interest of the Jewish people, it would be in the best interest of America.[218] He then told Harding that if it was at all possible he should speak with Lord Balfour about this matter.

Harding promptly agreed that speaking with Balfour would be a good political and strategic move and a moral gesture as well. This would also lead to a general understanding between the two powers that something coordinated between them should ensue, preferably sooner than later.[219] Glazer warned that if this coordination was later rather than sooner, Anglo-Saxon civilization would be doomed to utter destruction. To illustrate his point, Glazer told Harding that in the Slavic countries, Jews were persecuted in every facet of society. If good nations do not come to the rescue of the weak and innocent, they risked the continuity of their own civilization. Apparently taken aback by such a strong statement, Harding asked Glazer to elaborate. Glazer began to recount the story of the five orphaned children that had become homeless towards the end of World War I. Subsequently, Glazer was denied the right to adopt these children. According to Glazer, the story had a profound effect on Harding, which consequently, and most likely, swayed him to support the Zionist movement. It is important to briefly explain what Glazer related to Harding.

In 1911, a Jewish man from the Ukraine arrived in America without his family, settling in the state of Missouri. He had worked for several years, obtaining enough money eventually to send for his wife and five children. Before he could acquire the necessary paper work for them to immigrate to the United States, however, nine years had passed. In 1920, a group of Ukrainian soldiers had forced 2,000 Jews into the synagogue in Fastov, where they set the building on fire, killing all the Jews, including this man's wife. His children had gone to pick berries with their grandmother and escaped death that day. In the same year, the Jewish man in Missouri became an American citizen.

When news reached him that his wife had been horrifically burnt to death, the man became so ill that three days later he, too, had died.

This episode left his five children homeless and therefore orphaned. Glazer received a letter from the children asking that his wife be called "our mother" and that he be called "our father." Immediately after he received the letter, Glazer sought to adopt the five children, but his request was denied by the Immigration Department. Interrupting him, and noticeably moved, the President asked Glazer if he still wanted to adopt the children. Glazer replied in the affirmative and Harding told him that, by Executive Order, he would direct the Department of Immigration to immediately take care of the matter. He then asked Glazer to continue his thesis regarding the destruction of Anglo-Saxon civilization.

Glazer then proceeded to tell Harding that, because of such tragic incidents, the Jewish people needed a home of their own, where victims such as the orphaned children can find safe refuge. If nations do not recognize the need for justice, nor have the compassion to help children in dire straits, they are doomed to failure.[220] If a nation such as Ukraine, which had suffered so much in the previous seven years could yet turn a blind eye or even support such a murderous scheme against a minority people, religion or morality is certainly absent. Only in a country where religion is held sacred, such as the Anglo-Saxon civilization, can a world such as this be led to peace and harmony.

The President thanked Glazer for his description of the Jewish situation in the Russian and the former Austria-Hungarian region. Clearly, Glazer later notes, the President was genuinely moved, and fully understood the bleak situation of the Jews of Eastern Europe. He then proceeded to tell Glazer that if America could in any way help to stop the pogroms in that region or anywhere in the world for that matter, he would do so. This, he urged Glazer, to "tell his people."[221]

Glazer was so moved by the President's reply that he literally became speechless. He interpreted President Harding's message that the United States would eventually support a Palestine resolution calling for the creation of a Jewish homeland. To Glazer, the statement "if America could help in any away," meant that a Jewish state was "the only way" to solve the tenuous problem of the Jews. For clarification, Glazer then proceeded to ask Harding if he believed that the creation of a Jewish national home would prompt the cessation of atrocities against the Jews. Harding's answer shook Glazer: "Yes, I am fully convinced of that."[222]

Again, the President reiterated his commitment to personally meet with Lord Balfour as soon as there would be an opportunity to do so.

He stated that

> I shall talk to Mr. Balfour at my very earliest convenience,
> and I assure you that whatever lawful means America will be
> able to employ, we shall, with the help of God, do so to further
> the interest of your people in Palestine.[223]

Glazer then asked the President whether it would be wise to speak
with the State Department regarding the British, the Jews, and Palestine.
The President replied that he would definitely arrange a meeting with
Under-Secretary of State Fletcher, unless Secretary of State Hughes
was available.

The meeting between the President and the Rabbi lasted much
longer than the thirty minutes granted. At the conclusion, the President
called in his private secretary and instructed him to convey a message
to the Commissioner-General of Immigration and tell him that the five
orphaned children who had lost their parents be allowed immediate
access into the United States, to be under the care of Simon Glazer.
The final words of President Harding to Glazer were: "You may convey
to your people my greetings and my best wishes."[224]

In The Immediate Aftermath

Rabbi Glazer's meeting with President Harding appeared to produce the needed results. Not only was he able to convince, or have the President reaffirm that a Jewish national home was in the best interest of both the Jewish people and the United States, the President would also be the instrument of the world's redemption. Once the Jews had their home, as Glazer noted to Harding, the President would be recognized as *the* world leader who would guide the fractured planet to a time of peace and harmony.

When Glazer left the Executive Office of the President, the press, who had been eager to discover why he had spent so much time with Harding, bombarded him. Apparently, it was highly unusual that a meeting between the President and a lay leader last so long.[225] Following Glazer's exit from the White House, the President's secretary informed the press that the rabbi would be adopting five orphaned children from war ravaged Europe, and that a large part of their conversation revolved around this topic. However, absent from the Secretary's address to the press was the President's positive sentiments regarding the creation a Jewish national home. Glazer writes that the press had in fact been satisfied with the secretary's message, and some newspapers even published the story.[226]

During their meeting, Glazer told Harding that Arthur James Balfour was in Washington. Upon being notified that he was in the nation's capital, the President remarked that in his opinion Balfour had, for all time, secured his name in the annals of Jewish history.[227] Shortly thereafter, Harding in fact met with Balfour and, among other political discussions, expressed his wishes that Palestine become a homeland for the Jews. On November 21, three days after Glazer's meeting with Harding, Governor Allen, who was in Washington as well, wrote Glazer to inform him that he lunched with President Harding and Senator Curtis. Allen wrote that "They both spoke of you and of how glad they were to have an opportunity to comply with your request."[228]

Upon reading Allen's letter, Glazer concluded that he had removed all obstacles in the way for the United States to implement a resolution in favor of a Jewish national home in Palestine. Although still skeptical that such a resolution may actually be brought to a vote, he even asserted that the State Department would no longer be a hindrance to such a resolution. There remained one problem, however. Glazer points out in a letter to the Administrative Committee of the Zionist Organization of America (ZOA) that someone from the ZOA, allegedly one of their liaisons in Washington, had leaked to the press that Glazer had met with State Department officials in an attempt to convince them that a resolution be adopted by the United States supporting the Zionist endeavor. Upon learning of this leak, Glazer chastises a certain nameless "young man" who may have jeopardized his entire mission. Had the Syrians or the Arabians discovered his detailed plan, he writes, a course of counteractions against his mission would be inevitable. Glazer again stresses that the utmost secrecy of his mission be of prime importance.[229] He finished his letter by stating that though the possibility that the Syrians may have learned of his plan, he was not fearful of their attempts.[230] In fact, Glazer remained quite certain that he had succeeded in his mission:

> However, I rely upon God and have no fear of them or any of their clan, and have no doubt that, now with the attitude of the American government known the world over, Zionism will become reality; and if I had the least opportunity to do anything, I am only too happy to have been some service to such a cause. Respectfully submitted, Simon Glazer.[231]

Believing he was well on his way to accomplishing the goal that Chaim Weizmann commissioned him several months earlier, Glazer partially "turned the matter over to the Administrative Committee of the Zionist Organization of America."[232]

Consequently, the Zionist Organization of America contacted Senator Henry Cabot Lodge, the Republican Chairman of the Foreign Affairs Committee who had earlier promised to take the resolution, if ever drawn up, to the Senate Floor. Lodge, a trained historian, had been a supporter of the Judeo-Christian idea of the restoration of the Jewish people in their ancient homeland for years. He also had a history of working with the Jewish community of Massachusetts. The significance of an ally like Senator Lodge should not be underestimated. Lodge was one of the most powerful Senators in American history, particularly as the Chairman of the Senate Foreign Relations Committee, a body that he controlled for years (he was a Senator from 1893-1924). Most significantly he was the head of the Committee when President Woodrow Wilson, following World War I, attempted to get the Congress to ratify American involvement in the new League of Nations, as well as the Treaty of Versailles. Lodge strenuously opposed both, mainly because of his concern of American entanglement abroad, which the Versailles Treaty, he feared, would eventually lead to American entry into the League, and because of his distaste for Wilson. It is no understatement to note that Lodge, at least later in his career, was a major proponent of isolationism, and often clashed with Wilson's agendas (the two disliked each other).[233] His major apprehension with American involvement in the League of Nations, aside from the Versailles Treaty, was that it would eventually lead to American entanglements abroad and weaken the United States, something Lodge was perhaps correct about.[234]

Senator Lodge is considered the most responsible for the US Congress's negative position for the League of Nation ratification, and indeed, the League of Nations was established in 1920 without American participation. In 1918, to the consternation of Wilson, a Democrat, the House of Representative and the Senate was taken by the Republicans in a massive sweep, which catapulted Lodge from his already powerful position in the Senate Foreign Relations Committee to the Senate Majority Leader. In 1920, Lodge was one of a handful of Senators that both proposed and secured Warren G. Harding's nomination for President. It was during this time that he was approached by the Zionists to lend his support for the creation of a Jewish national home.

Although Senator Lodge had friends who were Jewish Republicans and who held positions in state government, it does not appear that they played a role, let alone a large role, in Lodge's support of Zionism. Lodge also had little reason to cater to the so-called "Jewish vote" or his Jewish base. In Boston alone, there had been about 77,000 Jews in 1920 and many of them poor and homeless.[235] He had no fear of losing the small percentage of the Jewish vote, approximately 10% of the city of Boston, and about 2% of the total state (similar to today). By the time he was approached to lend support to the Zionist movement Lodge had been a member of the Senate for nearly thirty years, and commanded respect from his Massachusetts constituents, and was friendly with the Jewish community. However, he did have difficulties in the 1922 election, and in 1917 many accused him of supporting initiatives for the wrong reasons, i.e. to get elected. For instance, many anti-Zionists did in fact level the charge again at Lodge that he was trying to win the Jewish vote, especially in 1922 because by that time he had alienated the "Irish and Catholic" blocks and therefore needed the Jews.[236] Although some have surmised this to be true, the fact is that Lodge supported the Balfour Declaration virtually from the onset of its issuance, and by 1919, while fighting to keep the United States out of the League of Nations, he issued a statement unbecoming of a so-called isolationist:

> I should be glad to see action by the United States in line with the Balfour Declaration. I feel that the efforts of the Jewish people to establish a national home in Palestine is not only natural but in all ways to be desired.[237]

It should be noted that Lodge had just been re-elected to the Senate and had no need to cater to the Jewish vote. His power, influence and potential intervention in the Massachusetts Legislative, as will be shown, had little to do with the "Jewish lobby". Lodge's home state of Massachusetts played a significant role in the eventual Federal government's state-sponsored Zionist position.[238]

Lodge appears to have readily agreed with the Zionist initiative. He also came to the conclusion that a Jewish state would be in the best interest of American foreign policy. In fact, shortly after the issuance of the Balfour Declaration, Lodge openly supported the endeavor.[239] Yet prior to agreeing to bring a pro-Zionist resolution to the Senate Floor, Lodge had several concerns that would have to be alleviated. The Senator, together with his team, had requested that numerous issues be detailed by the Zionist movement which could pose a confounding problem to US interests as interpreted by State Department officials. In particular, Lodge wanted a thorough explanation of the minutia of the Balfour Declaration. The Senator knew well that when the debate over of the Balfour Declaration transpired in England, many clauses, some seemingly more important than others, were debated and amended.[240] This might be equally true, he reasoned, and perhaps more so during the Congressional debate regarding the creation of a Jewish national home. Glazer, echoing Lodge's concerns, agreed.

In fact, Glazer had anticipated that this could be a potential future setback for the movement. Therefore, as a preemptive measure, Glazer drew up five elements he felt would be needed in order to satisfy all parties if the resolution ever made it to Congress.[241] Having thorough and straightforward answers to some of the most potent and logical questions against the creation of a Jewish national home, Glazer and his Zionist allies had a substantially better chance of convincing skeptical politicians to afford their support for Zionism. Incidentally, Glazer surmised that these answers may even bring skeptical Jews into the Zionist fold.

The first element that Glazer lists was the Jews presently living in Palestine. This included all Jews who had "local differences," i.e. those who were religious, secular, Ashkenazi and Sephardi. Many Jews, both from the New *Yishuv* and Old *Yishuv*, had varying opinions regarding the creation of a Jewish state, and often clashed.[242] Had the differences between the two sides not been rectified, many, including Glazer, feared that a split between the Jews of Palestine would resonate all the way to the halls of Congress. Of all places, if the Jews of Palestine could not find common ground in regards to the political aspects of their future, why would anybody, particularly the United States, support an endeavor that the Jews of the *Yishuv* did not?

The second element dealt with immigration, specifically those Jews who were migrating to Palestine from non-democratic countries. Glazer alluded to the State Department disapproving of Jews who support socialism, or "other brands of radicalism." Glazer knew that the United States was founded on the principles of liberty and freedom for all, ideas that communism, socialism, and also fascism (and later Nazism) often despised. Throughout history, particularly in the modern age, the leaders of such nations attempted to quell any sort of democratic change in their country. For the United States to support the creation of Jewish national home, it was essential that this future homeland be democratic, otherwise the chances for an independent Jewish state, at least supported by America, would be slim.[243] Glazer's task in this respect was to convince members of Congress that a future Jewish state would resemble American values, especially the most important one, freedom. As will shown, prior to any pro-Zionist ratification by the Congress, the Jews, both Zionist and non-Zionist, as well as the Arabs, debated these merits in front of numerous Congressional committees.[244]

The third element dealt with the Arab world as a whole. In particular, it was assumed by many in the State Department (and earlier in the British government) that, since the Arabs, and by extension Muslims, believe that Palestine is holy ground, this fact would inevitably be a cause of future problems between Mohammedan and Jew. Furthermore, many Jews also considered Palestine their Holy Land. Because both religions preach that the land is both holy and belongs to their respective faith and people, religious wars would be inevitable.

The Zionist movement, Glazer cautioned, must be able to counter this dangerous train of thought.

Glazer's fourth element dealt with the divergent ideological views found among world Jewry. He asked: How would the creation of a Jewish state affect the secular, anti-Zionists, ultra-Orthodox, and even those Jews who had (or were attempting) to assimilate? And what about those Jews, who, sympathetic to the plight of world Jewry, feared for their own well-being via citizenship in their respective countries, the ones who dreaded the charge of being labeled dual-loyalists? Glazer asserted that no Jew need fear if a Jewish state be created.

The fifth element dealt with political problems that would come in the wake of the creation of a Jewish national home. Similar to the third element that dealt with the Arab world's reaction to a "foreign occupier" inhabiting and controlling Muslim holy land, in the political sense, Glazer wondered how the Arab street would react to a resurrected Jewish nation. A major concern of the world powers, fueled by the obvious differences between Jewish and Arab religious, cultural and political institutions, was that the two sides would never get along.[245]

Glazer and Senator Lodge knew that the Congress, like the English parliament five years prior, would have to find answers to the noted quandaries if a resolution was to be passed. Yet one more point, not part of the five elements, yet so contentious and non-theoretical, that not to have a thorough and fair answer would jeopardize the Zionist movement's chances of a positive America resolution.

This final issue was the population differences between the Jews and Arabs of Palestine. Glazer was aware of some major discrepancies of Jewish versus Arab numbers. For instance, he writes, since the Arabs greatly outnumber the Jews, how could (or should) the Jews that number 80,000 control over 600,000 Arabs.[246] To counteract this position, Glazer asserts that land would not just be allocated to the Palestinian Jewish population, but to the entire Jewish Diaspora, numbering some 15 million. These numbers would easily offset the gap between the number of Jews and Arabs of Palestine.[247] Although interesting, many did not share this view.[248] The United States, and Great Britain before, opposed this train of thought. America and England would not view this "Zionist agenda" as legitimate policy. A major reason for the two nations' political leaders viewing this notion unfavorably – and Glazer appeared to agree – was their belief that the majority of world Jewry would not consider moving to Palestine even if a Jewish state was created. This perception evidently weakened the

Zionist movement's claim to the land of Israel.

Regardless, the noted elements would be explained to all who wanted to know how the Jews intended to govern their country. Following the positive feedback from Lodge, the next step prior to the Congress taking a closer look at supporting Zionism was to have a smaller body review and hopefully ratify an American version of the Balfour Declaration.

From Paris To Boston

For the following several years after World War I the Allies were busy trying to reformulate parts of war torn Europe. With the defeat and eventual collapse of the Ottoman Empire, as noted, lands throughout the near and Middle East that belonged to the Turks were divided among the victorious powers.[249] In May 1919, at the Paris Peace Conference, many of the Allied states met to discuss and ultimately resolve just exactly what to do with former Ottoman lands. It would not be until 1920, however, at the San Remo Conference, where representatives of the Supreme Council of the Allies, as well as other states (present was Great Britain, France, Italy, Greece, Belgium, and Japan) convened to discuss and ratify various points from the Paris Peace Conference a year earlier. On the agenda was the Treaty of Versailles, the peace treaty with Turkey, and among others, who to allot certain territorial areas of the Middle East.[250]

Blaringly absent from the San Remo Conference was the United States, though independently the US did confirm some of the San Remo issues, including the proposal that Great Britain become the Mandate holder of Palestine, and that the Balfour Declaration still be implemented. Prior to the Paris Peace Conference and San Remo, President Wilson was a sympathizer of the Balfour Declaration. He did not, however, issue a public statement of support even when the Balfour Declaration was first issued. Fearing that it might cause serious tension with Turkey, who at the time was not at war with the United States, Wilson heeded the calls of his staff until August of 1918. By that time Turkey's army had been decimated and Wilson was no longer fearful of Turkish antagonism.[251]

In 1919, prior to the Paris Peace Conference, Wilson had a slight slip of the tongue regarding his support for the British position and the status of Palestine, which left many Zionists speechless. In fact, when asked about the Balfour Declaration, Wilson remarked that the "foundation of a Jewish commonwealth" was possibly being prepared, and at the time was "under consideration by the British and Americans."[252]

Soon after Wilson made his remarks regarding a "Jewish commonwealth," an abundance of opposition soon followed, mostly from American Jews. Included in the list of dissenters, as noted earlier, were "thirty-one prominent American Jews" in total, such as *The New York Times* publisher, Adolph Ochs, diplomat Henry Morgenthau,

Morris Jastrow, professor of Semitic languages at the University of Pennsylvania, and twenty-eight others. Essentially the letter protested any political overtones regarding Palestinian Jewish colonization and politics.[253] Jastrow and others were afraid that the position of the Jews throughout the world would be endangered either by the creation of a Jewish state, or the mere public discourse concerning it, as many Jews throughout Europe still faced impending crises.

Indeed, Polish Jewry had continuously suffered by the hands of angry mobs. In an attempt to decipher the happening of 1918 and 1919, where scores of brutal pogroms were instituted against the Jews throughout Poland, Wilson appointed Morgenthau to investigate. His appointment served two purposes. The first major reason for his commission was to report on the situation of the Jews. The second was to send a message to the world that Wilson was not a major supporter of Zionism. By dispatching Morgenthau, a Jew and ardent opponent of political Zionism, though a champion of many Jewish causes, Wilson was playing both the Jews and other world bodies.

Appointing Morgenthau to head the investigative commission, against the vehement and unusual opposition of Jewish and Zionist American leaders sent a message about Wilson's "true" intent regarding the Balfour Declaration. When Morgenthau reported that the main reason for the massacres of Jews throughout Poland was because of nationalism – the Jews were upsetting the Polish nationals by displaying dual loyalties therefore they were being killed – it was clear to him that anti-Semitism *was not the* main factor for the pogroms. It was more of an issue of politics than Jew-hatred. Coming from such a prominent Jewish diplomat as Morgenthau, this allowed for the Wilson administration to back off, at least for the time being, with a public endorsement for the creation of a Jewish national home. Thus, more time was given for the Wilson administration to "study" Zionism and decide the best course of action for America to pursue.

At the Paris Peace Conference various other anti-Zionist ideas and documents surfaced, including the negative report of the King-Crane Commission. Henry Churchill King and Charles R. Crane were dispatched by Wilson to the Middle East initially to resolve certain territorial disputes between France and England, namely Syria.[254] However, shortly thereafter the Commission was sanctioned by Wilson to undertake an investigative analysis of the Arabs of Palestine, to the disappointment of the Zionists. Aside from recommending various changes to the American (and British) position regarding the formation of a potential future Jewish national home, later it was learned that King and Crane, who for the most part were opposed to Zionism, were told that "the Zionist" question in regards to the Allied Powers was virtually closed. That is, a Jewish state would eventually emerge.[255]

However, the Commission recommended that Palestine not be converted into a Jewish homeland, for among other issues, the Jews would create a powerful military force and displace the Arabs living there.[256] Although the findings weren't released until several years later (in 1922, ostensibly because of Jewish pressure), the Commission's findings, including the Polish conclusions, had been circulated at the Paris Peace Conference. The release of the Commission's reports only increased doubt among the foreign powers about the American commitment thus far to the Balfour Declaration and the creation of a Jewish national home altogether. Upon being questioned by Felix Frankfurter about the Commissions and their findings, President Wilson virtually said that his positive commitment to the creation of a Jewish national home in Palestine, though not official American policy at the time, should not be questioned.[257]

Following the closing of the Paris Peace Conference, which did not yield any fruit for Zionist endeavors, the San Remo Conference of 1920 would take a closer look at the Balfour Declaration. On April 24 of that year, the Conference officially gave England the Mandate over Palestine, and by July it was ratified in London. Most importantly for the Zionist movement, however, was the wording of the official Mandate. An excerpt of the 28 Articles of the Mandate reads as follows:

- Whereas the Principal Allied Powers have also agreed that the Mandatory should be responsible for putting into effect the declaration originally made on November 2nd, 1917, by the Government of His Britannic Majesty, and adopted by the said Powers, in favour of the establishment in Palestine of a national home for the Jewish people, it being clearly understood that nothing should be done which might prejudice the civil and religious rights of existing non-Jewish communities in Palestine, or the rights and political status enjoyed by Jews in any other country; and
- Whereas recognition has thereby been given to the historical connection of the Jewish people with Palestine and to the grounds for reconstituting their national home in that country.

It was the first time that many of the world's powers, excluding the United States, confirmed that a Jewish national home in fact be created.[258] Following the ratification of the British Mandate for Palestine in April 1920, the Zionist movement, under Chaim Weizmann, continued its forward progress. Shortly after the Mandate was given to England, Weizmann commissioned Rabbi Simon Glazer to lobby the US government and garner American support for the creation of a Jewish national home in Palestine. Once the leaders of Europe echoed England's position vis-à-vis the Balfour Declaration, the only world power left that mattered was the United States. It must have been reasoned by Weizmann and other Zionist leaders that, once most of the world's major powers supported Zionism in some form, the United States would follow. Only time would tell if this were to transpire.

In any event, once Glazer and Senator Lodge were convinced that official congressional approval for Zionism was opportune, particularly now that many of the world's powers agreed and partially committed to help the Zionist project succeed, American entanglement in Palestine would be minimal, if not beneficial for the United States. In March 1922, several months after Glazer's meeting with President Harding, a resolution was adopted in Lodge's hometown of Boston that called for the creation of a Jewish national home in Palestine. The Boston resolution was somewhat of a pilot project to see a) how the legislative body would react to such a resolution and b) what, after all negotiations, would the resolution read and c) if passed after debate, attempt to foresee how the US Congress would react. Lastly, the Boston resolution would be submitted to both Houses of Congress for a vote, and a copy would be sent to the President. On the request Elihu D. Stone, a Federal Assistant District Attorney, Zionist leader and former member of the State Legislature of Boston[259] (though it is likely that Senator Lodge played a role[260]) the Legislature of Massachusetts adopted the following joint State House of Representative and State Senate resolution.

- Order relative to recognizing Palestine as the homeland of the Jewish people.
- Whereas the Supreme Council of the Allied Peace Conference meeting at San Remo recognized the right of the Jewish nation to a national existence in Palestine and conferred upon Great Britain a mandate over Palestine; and
- Whereas the various great nations of the world approved the

establishment of the national homeland for the Jews in Palestine; and
- Whereas, the people of the United States, individually and through their spokesmen in Congress, and by leading men in all walks of life have expressed their gratification at the realization of the national hopes of the Jews; and
- Whereas the General Court of Massachusetts views with pleasure the progress of the Jewish people in Palestine in developing the economic resources of the country in founding institution of learning, and in creating a spiritual center so that it may better serve mankind.

Therefore be it

- Ordered, that the General Court of Massachusetts urges the Government of the United States of America formally to recognize the present status of the Jewish people in Palestine and thus to approve the fulfillment of this yearning desire for a national home in the land of its forefathers; and be it further
- Ordered, that copies of this order be sent by the Secretary of the Commonwealth, the President of the United States, to the presiding officers of both branches of Congress, to each of the Senators and Representative in Congress from Massachusetts and to the Zionist Organization of America.

In House of Representatives adopted March 29, 1922. In Senate adopted in concurrence, March 29, 1922.

W. Flood
Secretary of Commonwealth[261]

The Massachusetts Legislature unanimously passed the joint pro-Zionist resolution. The next day, on March 30, a fifteen-man Zionist delegation from Massachusetts, together with Speaker of the House Frederick H. Gillett, delivered the noted resolution from the Massachusetts General Court to Senator Lodge,[262] who subsequently asked the Senate to have the resolution printed in the Senate *Record* and referred to the Committee on Foreign Relations. One day later, on March 31, 1922 Lodge showed the resolution to Secretary of State Hughes.[263] It was said that Elihu Stone, one of Weizmann's and Glazer's confidants, convinced Lodge to bring it to the Senate Floor on the eve of Passover of that year. Stone said "this too would be an act of freedom for the Jewish people and Eretz-Israel."[264]

In some sense, the Boston resolution was needed in order to

strengthen Lodge's position within the Senate and State Department. Having a local, state legislative body debating and passing a resolution, as opposed to simply first having such a resolution brought to the Senate Floor, gave greater credibility to Lodge's case, and in some sense "cover". Lodge could state that the pro-Zionist resolution was indeed the will of his state citizens, as opposed to being a sole champion of the cause.

Within a few days, Lodge remarked to the Zionist delegation that he would bring a pro-Zionist resolution to the Senate Floor. In an interview on April 11, Lodge notified the Zionists that this resolution would be brought to the Floor "very shortly". In fact, the next day Lodge kept good on his word.

It is doubtful that Lodge would have brought a pro-Zionist resolution to the Senate Floor at this time had the major world powers and the political climate not adopted at least somewhat of a non-combatant approach towards the Balfour Declaration. After the Paris and then the San Remo Conference where England was granted the Mandate of Palestine and where the 28 Articles of the British Mandate for Palestine were issued, along with the Massachusetts State Legislature's positive endorsement of the Balfour Declaration, Lodge was ready to make a significant push for America to endorse the creation of a Jewish national home.

In The Chambers Of The Senate

Following the successful passing of the pro-Zionist resolution in the Massachusetts Legislature and Lodge's subsequent commitment to bring the resolution to the Senate Floor shortly thereafter, much work still remained. Glazer and Lodge anticipated a wide range of opposition to an American government sanctioned document supporting the creation of a Jewish national home in Palestine. Such opponents would most likely range from Americans who opposed US entanglement overseas, to the Arab world, including Palestine's Arabs who did not want the status quo altered. Additionally, Great Britain, who controlled the Mandate of Palestine and who issued the Balfour Declaration most likely did not want foreign interference in their affairs. Significantly as well, various Jewish groups, ranging from religious motives to the dual loyalists, also opposed Zionism. Each group, it was projected, might have to be pacified.

Although members of both the United States and the British government had their divergent view of what should constitute a future Jewish homeland, the Zionists equally differed from the American and English perspectives. This was, of course, understood by both sides. While the Zionist movement lobbied various world government officials to support the creation of a Jewish national home, it was anticipated that opposition to such a Jewish agenda would be stern. After all, the position of world Jewry at the time was politically weak, which remained so for decades to come (it was particularly weak through World War II). Regardless of the opposition or different visions, the Zionist movement believed that everything possible that can be done to build up the land of Israel be maximized. Glazer, too, echoed these sentiments. He believed that all endeavors that would help develop the *Yishuv* be organized and implemented correctly.

Specifically, Glazer notes that raising funds to purchase farming equipment should be a priority so that the Jews can prove to the nations, in particular Great Britain, that they can make a seemingly deserted, barren land blossom. While exclaiming the ability of the Jews to turn a depressed land into something thriving, or that which is "hopeless into hope", Glazer also cautioned that the Jews should not "waste good time in thinking of what Lord Northcliffe or anyone else will talk between tea and bedtime."[265] Even though England was often duplicitous when dealing with Zionism and many Brits were anti-Semitic, nevertheless

Glazer asserts that England would honor its pledge and implement the Balfour Declaration. He believed that an English commitment is virtually iron clad and, if promised, the Empire would make sure it happened "even to the last of his blood."

Glazer notes that if Palestine was threatened by an invading army, England would do all in its power, including deploying its soldiers from the ends of the earth, to ensure its honor was upheld. Since England promised that a Jewish homeland would be established, this commitment became "sacred ground." He wrote:

> From that sacred duty, England will not deviate. But it is necessary for all the Jewish people to know that we have no right to expect Palestine unless we also intend to re-consecrate its ground to the service of God and man. With this determination on our part, there will be little faulting with the proposed constitution.[266]

If America were to make a similar pronouncement and commit itself or lend its support for the establishment of a Jewish national home, a systematic lobbying plan would be needed. Hence, Weizmann's choice of Glazer. Without any political alliances, free of Washington's political taints, an Orthodox rabbi who simply believed that it was his religious duty to help anyway possible in the re-establishment of a Jewish state, Glazer was ideal. He was hard working, true to his cause and had allies.

Many of his friendship eventually opened doors where entrance was extremely difficult. Once Glazer had courted needed officials through his contacts that would have otherwise been virtually impossible without, more and more of his goal began to bear fruit. From the onset, Glazer believed that to convince the proper American government officials to support Zionism, a course of action complementary to that of England's leading up to the Balfour Declaration was mandatory. As the protectorate of Palestine only Great Britain had the power to decide Palestine's fate. However, Glazer and others reasoned that the United States could lend guidance and try to help to solve the Jewish problem of homelessness.[267]

While Lodge had now fully committed himself to the resolution, Glazer and the Zionist movement eagerly awaited the day that it was brought to the Senate Floor, and hopefully approved. When all of the contentious questions and answers were satisfactory to both Lodge and Glazer, the Zionist Organization of America continued contacting various politicians in the Congress for a hopeful endorsement of a pro-Zionist resolution, including one of their staunchest allies, Senator Charles Curtis.[268]

Meetings between Glazer and Curtis transpired months before the Massachusetts Legislature passed the pro-Zionist resolution and Lodge's commitment to bring a resolution to the Senate Floor. In a telegram dated December 12, 1921, Glazer implores Curtis to do all he could in assuring that the Senate introduce and pass the Palestine resolution.[269] He also requested that Curtis, if he had the time, meet with ZOA representatives at his convenience. Two days later, Curtis notified Glazer that he would not be able to meet. Like Senator Lodge who "is busy with the Conference (Disarmament Conference), where I (too) must be (there) at all times" as well.

Curtis did assure Glazer that he would meet with the rabbi's colleagues as soon as he had a chance.[270] Unfortunately, for Glazer and his ZOA team who were in Washington to meet with Curtis and Lodge, a meeting never took place. By the end of December, Glazer's delegation had left Washington.[271] At the end of the letter, however, Curtis informed Glazer that he hoped that his team will soon return to Washington, as he is "anxious to talk". Indeed, in mid January, Glazer's team did return to Washington and successfully met with Curtis, who once again committed himself to help the Jewish people to the best of his ability to create a home in Palestine.[272]

A brief word on Curtis's life history will help shed light as to possibly why he so heavily involved himself in the Zionist dilemma. Senator Charles Curtis of Kansas City, who later became Vice President of the United State (1929-1933), had a special sensitivity for the Jewish people. Perhaps he was a Philo-Semite, but certainly he was motivated to help the Jews acquire their homeland because of his own people's heritage. Curtis was the first Native American elected to the Senate in American history (1907).[273] As a persecuted minority for centuries, Native Americans, and in particular Senator Curtis, was most likely moved by the bleak situation of the Jews of Europe, particularly following World War I, where hundreds of thousands of Jews were killed or exiled. In the immediate aftermath of the war, a need for a Jewish national home became more desperate than ever, and certainly Curtis was cognizant of the desperate situation of the Jews.[274]

From January through April 1922 numerous meeting between Glazer, his team, and Senator Lodge and Curtis commenced. Yet following the Massachusetts Legislature's passing of the pro-Zionist resolution of March 1922, as well as Senator Lodge's commitment to bring the matter before the Senate, Glazer, Curtis, Lodge and their respective teams attempted to finalize all details of the potential resolution. By mid-April 1922 Senator Lodge had informed the Zionist leaders that the following day he was going to bring the Palestine Resolution to the Senate Floor.[275]

On April 12, 1922, Lodge kept good on his promise. The historic and monumental resolution he brought to the Senate Floor stated, among other revisions, the following:

> Resolved, etc. That the United States of America favors the establishment in Palestine of the national home for the Jewish people, it being clearly understood that nothing shall be done which many prejudice the civil or religious rights of non-Jewish communities in Palestine, and that the holy places and religious buildings and sites in Palestine shall be adequately protected.[276]

After months of exertion, Glazer and his team succeeded in getting the Zionist question before a large part of the American government. However thus far was accomplished, there was still much work to be done. A vote in the Senate was to be taken within one month of the Palestine resolution's introduction. Furthermore, the Zionist movement needed the House of Representatives to also endorse the proposal, which in turn would then have to be brought to the President for his support. Otherwise, if only both houses of Congress supported the resolution while the President did not, it would have meant that the Zionist initiative was an "unqualified commitment" of the United States, i.e. it would have no practical effect. Following the Senate introduction of the Palestine resolution, an immediate concern was the major task of convincing the House of Representatives and the President to officially support the cause.

The Month Of Deliberations In The Senate And House Of Representatives

The Palestine Lodge Resolution that the Senate put forth was a milestone achievement for the Zionist movement. Although the resolution had not been passed, or yet debated, the mere fact that it was brought before the Senate was meaningful and productive. Lodge, who at the time was at his height of his isolationist rhetoric and policy, stood little to gain politically by supporting what was conceived as a highly polarized issue from a variety of peoples and governments, including the Jews themselves.

Although the Zionist movement, and in particular Glazer, had been attempting to garner Senate support, Congressman Hamilton Fish Jr., of New York, decided on his own initiative to bring the question of American support for a Jewish national home to a vote in the House of Representatives. As early as April 4, 1922, a little more than a week before Lodge's introduction, Congressman Fish introduced a resolution of sympathy for Zionism to the House Floor.[277] The initiative would have put the House of Representatives on record for sanctioning the "undertaking" of the creation and restoration of the Jewish people in their ancient homeland. Fish's text read as follows:

> Whereas, the Jewish people have for many centuries believed in and yearned for the rebuilding of their ancient homeland, and whereas, owing to the outcome of the World War, and their part therein, the Jewish people, under definite and adequate international guarantees are to be enabled with due regard to the rights of all elements of the population of Palestine and the sanctity of its holy places, to re-create and reorganize a national home in the land of their fathers;

> Therefore be it

> Resolved by the House of Representatives (the Senate concurring) that the Congress of the United States hereby expresses its profound satisfaction in that outcome of the victorious war which promises the building up of a new and beneficent life in Palestine, rejoices in this act of historic justice

about to be consummated, and on behalf of the American people commends[278] an undertaking which will do honor to Christendom and give to the House of Israel its long-denied opportunity to reestablish a fruitful Jewish life and culture in the ancient Jewish land.[279]

Although the document is also historical in the sense that it is the first official House of Representatives attempt to support Zionism, it fell short of what many had hoped for, namely the wording or sentiments found in the Balfour Declaration. The House resolution did not have the same positive reception that the Senate version received.

The Zionists, though pleased that Congressman Fish would initiate such a process, were somewhat disappointed. Sanctioning an "undertaking" for the creation of a Jewish national home was far below Senator Lodge's recommendation, and it was feared that getting the House to amend the resolution would be difficult. Lodge had called for the "establishment of the National Home" for the Jewish people in their ancient land.[280] It would be a challenging month for the Zionist movement to convince both the House of Representatives that Fish's resolution needed to be stronger, and that pieces of Lodge's resolution be amended. However, Fish was adamant about the Resolution being passed and worded correctly. He said:

> Mr. Speaker, this resolution favors the establishment in Palestine of a national home for the Jewish people and is based on justice and humanity. It has been given full consideration in the Committee on Foreign Affairs and that committee has reported it out practically unanimously. It is almost similar in wording to a resolution passed a month ago in the other branch of the legislative body. The only difference is that we changed the word "the" to the word "a" so that instead of its reading "the national home" it reads "a national home." The House has had this matter under consideration for the past week and members are familiar with the contents of the resolution.

> The passage of this resolution does not commit us to an entangling alliance or to any obligation to use military or naval force or the expenditure of any money. It is merely an expression of our sympathetic and favorable attitude in establishing in Palestine a refuge for the persecuted Jews of the world where

they can develop their own culture, law, and ideals in the ancient land of their fathers, given by Jehovah to Abraham and consecrated in the hearts of the Jewish people as the birthplace of their traditions.

This resolution has nothing to do with the League of Nations or the mandatory power under the league. We are not a party to the league, and it would be a piece of impertinence for us to attempt to dictate to the membership of the league. Those who are for or against the league, reservationists and irreconcilables all alike, and support this resolution with equal fervor, as it expresses the moral encouragement of the Congress of the United States to a project already endorsed by Great Britain, France, Italy, Japan, and other great nations. I append hereto a copy of House Joint Resolution 322 and a copy of the report.[281]

Shortly after Fish's introduction of a pro-Zionist resolution it was referred to the House Committee on Foreign Affairs, which consisted of fourteen Republicans and six Democrats, of which Adolph I. Sabbath of Chicago was the only Jew.[282] The Foreign Affairs Committee decided to hold hearings on the resolution, unlike their counterparts in the Senate. A sub-committee of three, with Fish as the head, was tasked to see to it that the resolution makes its way through the House. The hearings were set to take place between April 18 and April 21, 1922.

In regards to the Senate, Lodge took a more methodical and cautious approach than Fish during the month of April. Specifically, he did not introduce the resolution to the Senate Floor until he had the unanimous approval of the Senate Foreign Relations Committee, the body that he chaired.[283] Indeed, the process from Lodge's introduction on April 12 through May 3, the day that the Senate approved the Zionist proposal, was a time where the Senator's influence was paramount. Lodge did secure a unanimous vote on his committee, where twelve out of the sixteen members voted for the Palestine Resolution, one was recorded as "favoring" it, while the remaining three Senators were absent.[284]

The text that was passed on April 12 was amended, so that by May 3, when the vote in the Senate came, it read the following:

Resolved, etc. That the United States of America favors the establishment in Palestine of the national home for the Jewish people, it being clearly understood that nothing shall be done which may prejudice the civil or religious rights of non-Jewish communities in Palestine, and that the holy places and religious buildings and sites in Palestine shall be adequately protected.[285]

Glaringly absent from the above resolution is any mention of the Balfour Declaration. Lodge attempted to assuage the fears of those who believed that endorsing the Balfour Declaration would be construed as an indirect ratification of the League of Nations, particularly since the Balfour Declaration formed a part of the League's mandate.[286] Even the mere perception of American entanglement abroad led many Senate and House leaders to take a cautionary approach regarding any endorsement of the creation of a Jewish national home in Palestine. However, the Zionist movement, though cognizant of the difference in wording, cared little. The fact was the resolution called for the establishment of the national home for the Jewish people.

Lodge's new resolution omitted the phrase "or the rights and political status enjoyed by Jews in any other country", wording found in the Balfour Declaration. Those Jews who opposed Zionism, or were non-Zionist, protested the omission. The Zionists dismissed the exclusion as being "gratuitous and supererogatory", at least as far as American Jewry was concerned.[287] *The New York Times*, however, believed that

> ...all Jewish non-Zionists of this country are aroused, not so much by the omission of the words holding inviolate their rights in other countries, but by the very fact that suspicion is aroused by their deletion.[288]

However much angst was issued over this omission it had little to no effect on the text of the resolution. Once Lodge reported to the Senate that he intended to bring forth a resolution supporting the creation of a Jewish national home in Palestine, he changed some of his tactics. Lodge asked the Senate for permission to suspend the normal rules and procedures and bring the resolution for immediate consideration and vote. Lodge's requests were granted. On May 3, 1922, the Senate, without debate, unanimously approved the pro-Zionist resolution, referred to as the Palestine Lodge Resolution.[289]

Although the Zionist movement was energized by this unanimous approval, there was much to be done. The next step, of course, was to convince the House of Representatives that the passing of a pro-Zionist resolution would be both a moral and practical gesture for the United

States. To aid in the endeavor of convincing skeptical Congressmen to support Zionism at this critical time, the Zionists employed a tactic that Glazer had created in his hometown of Kansas City. Aside from the creation of the Pro-Judaea of the Midwest that Glazer established, which consisted of a body of influential businessmen, clergymen and political figures, the Zionist movement also created various groups to help in their quest. In the forthcoming days, when Fish's resolution was to be debated in the House, the Zionists employed the "Society of Friends of a Jewish Palestine" that, like the Pro-Judaea, was made up of only Christian patrons that was specifically created to garner support for the creation of a Jewish national home in Palestine.[290] As noted earlier, the reason for the formation of the Pro-Judaea as well as groups such as the Society of Friends of a Jewish Palestine was to gather support from mainstream Christians, who in turn would help in the raising of funds for Zionist activity. However, for this particular juncture they would help lobby government officials. So important was the utilization of these organizations that Abraham Goldberg (Secretary of the Palestine Bureau and member of the Administrative Committee of the ZOA) remarked that only with such non-Jewish organizations can the Zionists "counter-act all these (anti-Semitic) calumnies in England, as well as in this country (United States)." As in England prior and subsequent to the Balfour Declaration, American Zionism needed a non-Jewish, pro-Zionist campaign. Zionist dissension, Goldberg and others asserted, needed the full attention of the American Jewish community and Christian help to counteract the negative propaganda that was being spread by the enemies of the Jews.[291]

It would not be known until the end of April 1922 if this Zionist counter-offensive positively materialized. Many factors were at play. The Senate was awaiting House ratification. If the House passed a pro-Zionist motion, Lodge would then initiate a joint-Congressional initiative. This would entail the creation of a new resolution where both Houses of Congress would have to agree on the wording. However, before such a joint resolution could be considered, a heated debate in the House of Representatives that brought Arabs, non-Zionists, anti-Zionists, Orthodox Jews, Reform Jews, and plain Zionists to the Chambers left many Congressmen in disarray.

The Debate In The House Of Representatives

In some respect, Congressman Hamilton Fish Jr. shared a similar view of Zionism as Senator Lodge. Both men believed that the creation of a Jewish national home was in the best interest of the United States and both fought passionately for American recognition of the Balfour Declaration, or those terms stated in the proclamation. However, Lodge and Fish also believed that the United States should remain neutral in foreign affairs, and in no way get caught up in foreign entanglements, especially since World War I was so costly. Which, of course, begs the question: If they were such staunch advocates of American isolationism, why support the establishment of a Jewish state or even get involved in the first place?

Lodge's view regarding American support for a Jewish national home, as stated earlier, rested on two foundations. The first was his Christianity and humanitarianism, which could be one and the same. As Jesus was a Jew and the Jews were the Chosen People (not to mention he held evangelical beliefs regarding the Second Coming of Christ), he may have felt that it was his duty to support the Zionist cause. The second reason, vaguer though, was because he believed a Jewish national home in the Middle East would be good for the United States. He envisioned – though he did not elaborate – that a Zionist state would be an ally of America.

Congressman Hamilton Fish's reasons for supporting Zionism appear to be more obscure than Lodge's. Fish was elected to the House of Representatives in the Republican takeover of 1920. His hometown of Dutchess County, New York had a small Jewish population, and, like Lodge's, would not be a decisive factor for his reelection. Meaning, he too would not have to cater to the "Jewish vote." However, his critics, who included the periodical *The American Hebrew*, asserted otherwise. True, Fish had no reason to court the Jewish vote of his district, at least for the House. Yet his detractors believed that Fish was playing the Jewish card for a potential future run for the Senate, which is why, many claim, he supported a pro-Zionist resolution.[292]

In April 1922, when Fish introduced the resolution to the House he had only been a freshman congressman, with little seniority. Yet his power was increasing. However, the longer Fish was in office the more negative accusations were leveled his way. For instance, not long after he sponsored the resolution he was accused of being a

Nazi sympathizer, one who espoused the "America firster" approach (close the borders), and by extension of both, an anti-Semite.[293] Of course Fish denied the first and third charges (Nazi sympathizer and anti-Semite) as being absurd. True, he remarked, he was opposed to communism and its spread as well as American involvement overseas, and believed that American interests came first. Although he had his skeptics, *The American Hebrew* and other periodicals were historically proven wrong regarding the Congressman's intentions. He never did run for Senate, and in fact served the House of Representatives and his district for twenty-five years.

In regards to Fish's introduction of the pro-Palestine resolution, the Congressman claimed that he initiated it for a number of reasons. The first he mentions was because he was inspired by the Zionist dream. This factor perhaps was the main catalyst for Fish's support. He in fact brought the resolution on his own initiative, and as noted, did not need to cater to the Jewish vote of his district. It is also surmised that a good part of Fish's support for the creation of a Jewish national home was inspired by a certain Jew, Henry Holtzmann of Brooklyn, New York. Fish and Holtzmann were very close friends, which may have played a role in the Congressman's support for Zionism.[294]

Additionally, aware of the plight of Eastern European Jewry during and subsequent to World War I, where, as noted, the Jews suffered tremendous loss of life and land, Fish was moved by compassion. Further, Fish was also an evangelical Christian and was possibly moved to support the creation of a Jewish national home for messianic purposes. The aforementioned, in one form or another, can be viewed in Fish's opening remarks when the Congressional Committee began the Palestine resolution hearings.[295] In Fish's own words, he said that

> This report expresses our moral interest in and our favorable attitude toward the establishment in Palestine of a national home for the Jewish people. It commits us to no foreign obligations or entanglement. The protection of the holy places is carefully provided for, as well as the rights of Christian and all non-Jewish communities. There is a strong religious and humanitarian appeal in this recognition accorded to the Jewish people that goes beyond its purely material aspects and the discharge of such obligations assured by the allied governments as expressed by the Balfour Declaration of November 2, 1917, which has been endorsed by France, Italy, Japan, and other nations. The

Jews of America are profoundly interested in establishing a national home in the ancient land for their race. Indeed, this is the ideal of the Jewish people everywhere, for despite their dispersion Palestine has been the object of their veneration since they were expelled by the Romans. For generations they have prayed for the return to Zion. During the past century this prayer has assumed practical form...[296]

The Committee on Foreign Affairs of the House of Representatives commenced its debate on April 18, 1922 amid speculation that a plethora of groups would vehemently protest the House's decision regarding its proposed pro-Zionist resolution. In fact, it had originally been Fish's intent just to bring the Palestine resolution to the House Floor for a vote without deliberation (like Lodge), but once word reached the opponents of such an initiative they demanded that a debate be allowed to ensue. Literally, in haste, the hearings were arranged overnight.[297]

Over the course of the next few days fourteen people testified in front of the House Committee, the majority being supporters of Zionism. They included such figures as Louis Lipsky, Abraham Goldberg, Elihu D. Stone, Dr. Herman Seidel (president of the Maryland Palestine Foundation Fund), four Congressmen who essentially read resolutions endorsing the creation of a Jewish national home in Palestine,[298] and Morris Lazaron, a Reform non-Zionist rabbi.

The opposing parties were from the Reform movement, and included two rabbis, David Phillipson of Cincinnati, Ohio and Isaac Landman of Long Island, New York. Three other individuals who testified were Dr. Edward B. Reed of Yale University who was Deputy Commissioner for the Red Cross in Palestine for three and a half months in 1919, and two American Arabs of Palestinian origin, Selim Totah, a law student in Washington, and Fuad Shatara, a physician living in Brooklyn.

As the head of the Committee, Fish opened his remarks with a restatement of the resolution as well as its implied practicality. He notes that the resolution "is purely a moral expression of the favorable attitude of Americans towards a Jewish homeland and commits us to no foreign obligations or entanglements."[299] However, it was clear from previous statements, and indeed his introductory tone, that Fish wanted committee members to hear the Zionist perspective and then call for an immediate vote. This though would not materialize. What followed was no less than one hundred and seventy pages of testimony from both Zionist and anti-Zionist witnesses, portraying the emotional impact of the proposed resolution.

The Zionists brought forth numerous arguments why America should support the creation of Jewish national home. Below is a list of Zionist talking points.

• The approval and implementation of the Balfour Declaration and the Palestine mandate is critical in order that the Jews of Europe be given a refuge.

• The vast majority of American Jewry favors and supports the Zionist goals.

• The anti-Zionists constitute a small fraction of American Jewry who are insensitive to Jewish life and its problems.

• The Allied powers, including President Wilson, followed by President Harding supported the Balfour Declaration.[300]

• The vast majority of American Jews would not pick up and leave for Palestine, as they had prosperous lives and lived in complete freedom.

• Zionism was completely compatible with patriotism and Americanism.

• Zionist and Jewish settlement in Palestine would greatly enhance the quality of life of both Arab and Jew currently in Palestine.

• Arab property would not be expropriated.[301]

Many of the noted arguments had been used for years by Zionist groups when trying to garner both British and American support for the establishment of a Jewish national home. The cited talking points virtually covered every argument of the Zionist movement, save the most contentious one, that of the Jewish and Arab population differences. Regardless, a home for the Jews fit in with American ideals: The movement strove to be free, to be a refuge for persecuted peoples, it was compatible with American philosophy, and the Jews will respect the rights of the inhabitants living there.

The arguments presented against the Zionists were also numerous, and somewhat strong, though they did not resonate through the Congress. Reed, the two Arab witnesses and the two rabbis stated their opposition with a number of points as well.

• The Zionist program seeks to oppress the Arabs, or at the very least will oppress the Arabs, who are the majority of Palestine's inhabitants.

- The Zionist program is illegal and violates Arab rights.
- The United States would be drawn into an approval of the League of Nations mandate through the adoption of a pro-Zionist resolution.
- Jewish nationalism was a myth perpetuated by the mandate and the Balfour Declaration. Rabbi Philipson remarked "America is my national home."[302]
- The persecution of the Jews will not stop just because they have a homeland. Only when the entire world is free will the Jews cease being persecuted.

The reactions of the Committee members to the three Reform rabbis varied. Rabbi Lazaron, the non-Zionist rabbi, was pleased when Fish introduced an addition to the resolution that morning, namely that "non-Jewish communities in Palestine and the political status of the Jews in the Diaspora" be protected. Rabbi Landman, who opposed the resolution, remarked that he wasn't opposed to Palestine being colonized by persecuted Jews, just that no talk of Jewish nationalism should ever be heard.[303] Citing the Zionist Organization of America's statistic that only 30,000 members are part of the organization, Landman stated that with so few numbers, one could not claim that American Jewry was Zionistic. In fact, he continued, many American Jews support the upkeep of the Jewish community there, but many do not support its nationalistic ambitions.

The Reform movement's position on Zionism had been well known by the time the hearings commenced. Rabbis Philipson and Landman both gave an overview of the Reform position from 1897, with the convening of the first Zionist Congress in Basel, to 1922.[304] The official Reform position during those years was mainly consistent. In the 1885 Pittsburg Platform, the first major initiative by American Reform to codify their tenets, it stated that the Jews "no longer constitute a nation" and therefore there is no need for a Jewish home again.[305] In 1890, in a conference in Cleveland, the movement went on record again – this time theologically – that denied any more a Jewish desire or need to return to Palestine or of Jewish nationalism.[306] The movement, however, would be tested in 1897 with Herzl's call for a Jewish state, where many Jews were intrigued by the Basel Conference. In response to Herzl, the Central Conference of American Rabbis, led then by Isaac Meir Wise, an American Reform leader, decried any form of Jewish nationalism.

Resolved, That we totally disapprove of any attempt for the establishment of a Jewish state. Such attempts show a misunderstanding of Israel's mission...Such attempts do not benefit, but infinitely harm our Jewish brethren where they are still persecuted, by confirming the assertion of their enemies that the Jews are foreigners in the countries in which they are at home...We reaffirm that the object of Judaism is not political nor national, but spiritual...[307]

Reform statements opposing Jewish nationalism were reiterated several times through 1922, such as in 1906 in Indianapolis and 1912 in Baltimore.[308] However, in 1917, in response to the Balfour Declaration, Dr. William Rosenau, President of the Central Conference of the Reform movement, the main Reform government body, issued the following statement.

We herewith reaffirm the fundamental principle of Reform Judaism, that the essence of Israel as a priest people, consists in its religious consciousness, and in the sense of consecration to God and service in the world, and not in any political or racial national consciousness. And therefore, we look with disfavor upon the new doctrine of political Jewish nationalism, which finds the criterion of Jewish loyalty in anything other than loyal to Israel's God and Israel's religious mission.[309]

Reform restatements opposing the establishment of a Jewish state could be heard in 1919 during the Paris Peace Conference as well as in 1920 after the San Remo Conference, and in the 1922 Congressional hearings.[310]

The aforementioned resolutions by the Central Conference of American Rabbis were cited by Rabbi Philipson during his testimony before the House Committee. Philipson, who for years had opposed any form of Jewish nationalism, told the Committee that the Zionists had misinterpreted Jewish literature. For years, he said, the Jews had ceased to be a nation and therefore there was no longer any need for the establishment of a Jewish national home. The only thing the Zionists have accomplished thus far, he continued, was an increase in the level of anti-Semitism and a worsening of the Jewish situation. Philipson also emphasized that American support for the establishment of a Jewish national home is tantamount to the United States committing itself to foreign involvement. Lastly, Philipson remarked that the government should not involve itself in an entirely internal religious affair.[311]

Most importantly, however, Philipson wanted Congress to understand that "Zionists do not speak for all Jews."[312] Some of Philipson's sentiments were retold by members of Congress during their internal debate over the resolution. Congressman Walter M. Chandler, who was a stanch supporter of the resolution, singled out Philipson's views for debate, even though he did not believe the majority of Philipson's constituency, Reform Jews, agreed with him or the Reform movement's anti-Zionist position.[313] Philipson said that

> We are unalterably opposed to political Zionism. The Jews are not a nation but a religious community. Zion was a precious possession of the past, the early home of our faith, where our prophets uttered their world subduing thoughts, and our psalmist sang their world enchanting hymns. As such it is a holy memory, but it is not our hope of the future. America is our Zion. Here, in the home of religious liberty we have aided in founding this new Zion, the fruition of the beginning laid in the old. The mission of Judaism is spiritual, not political. Its aim is not to establish a State, but to spread the truths of religion and humanity throughout the world.[314]

Concerned over Reform aspirations and their influence, Rabbi Glazer jumped into the debate. He informed members of Congress, including Senator Charles Curtis that the Reform position has no validity. Glazer stated that less than three percent of world Jewry maintained that such a resolution should not be issued, while ninety-seven percent supported such a proclamation. Members of the Reform movement, he wrote, were afraid that all of world Jewry would be segregated into one area, like a ghetto. Glazer, echoing Philipson's position, eluded to a conversation he once had with Senator Curtis where he explained that Reform Jews had abrogated all contact with the land of Israel, maintaining that Jerusalem is a state of mind. Therefore the physical location of the holy city became obsolete. Upset that such a movement among Jews was negatively influencing Senators and Congressmen regarding support for the Palestine resolution, Glazer reminded members of Congress that a Jewish home would save tens of thousands of lives.[315] Many members of Congress, including Senator Lodge and Curtis, told Glazer that they would do all in their power in "securing early action."[316]

The most astute anti-Zionist witness was Dr. Edward Reed of Yale.[317] Aside from being the Deputy Commissioner of the Red Cross in Palestine for several months in 1919, he was well versed in Zionist affairs. Reed testified at the hearings that he had originally supported Zionism. However, upon acquainting himself with the Arab inhabitants of the land he changed his mind. Reed felt that the Arabs would be displaced by the Jews, or in a more combative tone, the Zionists will usurp the land. Although he recognized that the Balfour Declaration was intended for good, the consequence of such an implementation would be that the Jews, who only constitute 10% of Palestine's population, would control the other 90% of the inhabitants, the Arabs. This, Reed remarked, was wholly un-American, which incidentally went against the American doctrine of self-determination, and therefore could not be supported.

Reed further testified that Lodge's Resolution had gone too far. It was one thing, he argued, if the Balfour Declaration stated that "*a* national home" for the Jewish people be established. For "*a* national home" left the question of how large this home would be. However, the Lodge Resolution stated that Palestine should become "*the* national home" for the Jewish people, potentially alienating many Jews who were non-Zionist, and most importantly, implying that the entirety of Palestine should encompass the Jewish home.

In an editorial of *The New Palestine*, Reed was accused of being an Arab agent.[318] However, he claimed that he held no bias towards either Arab or Zionist, just that the facts spoke for themselves. At the hearings, Reed maintained that he paid his own way while in Washington, though it surfaced – and he later admitted– that he brought Totah and Shatara, the two Arabs who testified, to the hearings. In addition, at the committee hearing, Reed testified that the Zionists were to blame for the prolonged conflict of World War I,[319] language that the many a Zionist and Congressman noted echoed the Protocols of the Elders of Zion, the late 19th Century anti-Semitic forgery that claimed the Jews were conspiring to conquer and dominate the world.[320]

Totah and Shatara testified that the Arabs of Palestine were perfectly capable of developing the landscape and agriculture of the land. The Jews who came to Palestine, they argued, were not adequately trained in cultivation and in fact had mostly employed Arabs to work the land. The Zionists were simply unable to be self-sufficient, he maintained, and in the long-term would be unable to maintain existence without

Arab help. Aside from the statements rendering Jewish development obsolete without Arab labor, Totah and Shatara charged that the Jews were the agents of Bolshevism,[321] and had caused the 1921 Jaffa riots.[322]

Totah and Shatara concluded their remarks by stating that is was "they", the Arabs, who really "owned" the land. It was important to understand, they stated to the Committee, that the Jews could not be self-sustaining, let alone build a nation. However, the fact was, they concluded, the Arabs of Palestine were descended from the ancient Philistines who had never left the land. Two thousand years ago, when the Jews were exiled (from Judaea), they ceased being a nation.

For the most part, the anti-Zionist arguments fell on deaf ears. The Committee was run by Congressman Fish (and William Bourke Cockran of New York as well), an ardent supporter of Zionism and of the Congressional resolution. Louis Lipsky and Abraham Goldberg, it was reported, had a "stabilizing" effect on the Committee.[323] They pointed out that the United States had tentatively agreed to help establish a Jewish homeland, and that the Committee could help by lending its moral support for the cause.

Lipsky and Goldberg were able to present their case in a systematic fashion. Not only was the Zionist cause worthy of American government support in 1922, they reasoned, it was even recognized years prior by previous Congressmen and Presidents. As early as 1919, the Zionist track record for garnering American support was impressive. In that year, the movement had collected over three hundred signatures from Senators and House of Representative members supporting the Balfour Declaration.[324] The anti-Zionist witnesses at the Committee hearing could claim no such track record.

In the end, Congressman Fish directed the hearings to foster a pro-Zionist mood, and indeed, most members of the Committee favored the Zionist position. Two things were apparent in the House Committee's favorable view of Zionism. The first was the humanitarian position. The Jews of Eastern Europe had recently been decimated during World War I with nowhere to turn. They faced impending political and physical persecution in their "home" states. Not to support the Zionist cause would have left the impression that the Congress was "anti-humanitarian," a charge that was to be avoided at all cost. The second factor that played a role in many House members' support of the pro-Zionist resolution was the belief that most American Jews supported Zionism, a belief that the Zionist movement may have invented or more likely embellished. By supporting Zionism, as some asserted, many Congressmen would gain needed favor in their districts with large Jewish populations.[325]

Following the hearings Fish was convinced that the members of the Committee agreed with the Zionist position. However, he did not want to formally bring the resolution to a vote in the House until the Senate had voted on its resolution. Although Fish believed that the Senate would pass a pro-Zionist resolution, he wanted Lodge to use his influence and garner additional support in the House. If the Senate passed the resolution, Fish believed that he would have an easier chance obtaining ratification in the House. By the end of April 1922, both Fish and Lodge were ready for each Congressional branch to vote on the Palestine proposals, something the Zionist movement eagerly anticipated.

Independent Congressional Resolutions

With the closing of the Congressional hearings in late April 1922 the Zionists were confident that a pro-Zionist resolution would pass in both Houses of Congress. However, even though much had been accomplished, many in the movement feared that the text of the document could be greatly watered down to appease those who opposed a pro-Zionist position. Absent from the hearings in the House of Representatives was any official from the Department of State, the most vocal and consistent American opponent of both the Balfour Declaration and Zionism altogether. It would only be days later, following the closing of the hearings, that State Department officials would voice their concerns and leverage their power to dissuade any passing of a pro-Zionist resolution in the Congress and later with the Harding administration.

Senator Lodge and Congressman Fish knew that there would be branches of government opposed to such a Congressional resolution. Both men conferred with each other about the exact wording of the proposed text with the intent that, if and when the resolution would be jointly agreed upon, the most expeditious procedure be employed. Partially, that was in response to any unforeseen opposition. In fact, on April 18, 1922, Fish submitted to the Congress a joint resolution (House Joint Resolution 307) calling for the "recreation of Palestine as the national home of the Jewish race."[326]

Fish's reasoning for introducing this joint resolution – one of numerous resolutions thus far – was that it would require the President's signature to hold any valuable weight. By introducing a joint Congressional resolution, the document would be much more influential than if only sanctioned by one branch. As for the reason he placed "Jewish race" in the text, it was to appease Rabbi Landman, one of two anti-Zionist Reform rabbis who testified. On the same day that Fish submitted House Joint Resolution 307, he also introduced the Massachusetts Legislature's pro-Zionist resolution from March 1922 to the House. This, he felt, would bring a certain positive mood to the House chambers, hopefully one of acquiescence. Additionally, by showing the Massachusetts Legislature's resolution, Fish, like Lodge, could show that a more grass-roots body already took up the issue of a Jewish national home and positively endorsed it.

However, on the following day, April 19, Fish submitted a new document that replaced "Jewish race" with "the Jewish people," most likely in response to the Zionists who did not want such a phrase used. Senator Lodge and Congressman Fish then met with Secretary of State Hughes to go over the text and to discuss what had thus far transpired. Hughes approved of Lodge's resolution (apparently orally) while Fish was told to change certain features of his text before the Secretary would grant his approval.[327] Fish, in fact, did change the document numerous times over the course of the next several months.

Following the House Committee hearings, which approved Fish's resolution, the Congressman would have to choose a pro-Zionist text that would be fitting to submit for official sponsorship. He again sought the council of Senator Lodge, and on May 3, 1922, Fish introduced yet another version of the Palestine resolution (House Joint Resolution 322) that would hopefully be passed.

> Whereas owing to the outcome of many centuries the Jewish people believed in and yearned for the rebuilding of their ancient homeland
>
> and
>
> Whereas, owing to the outcome of the World War and their part therein, the Jewish people are to be enabled to recreate and reorganize a national home in the land of their fathers which will give to the House of Israel its long-denied opportunity to re-establish a fruitful Jewish life and culture in the ancient Jewish land, therefore be it
>
> Resolved etc., that the USA favors the establishment in Palestine of the national home for the Jewish people, it being clearly understood that nothing shall be done which may prejudice the civil and religious rights of Christians and all other non-Jewish communities in Palestine, and that the holy places and religious buildings and sites in Palestine shall be adequately protected.[328]

While the introduction was modified the basic part of the resolution, that being anything after "Resolved," was almost identical to Lodge's proposal. Even as Fish was busy amending the proposal and attempting to secure approval for his new version, the Senate, on the same day, was about to consider "Joint Resolution 191". Lodge, however, had requested that three amendments be considered to the text:

1) delete the clause referring to the Balfour Declaration;

2) delete the word "existing" in the statement "existing non-Jewish communities in Palestine";

3) exclude the phrase that referred to the Jews of the Diaspora.

Lodge succeeded in getting the amendments implemented, but some questioned the rationale. For instance, the removal of any indication of the Balfour Declaration, it was stated, was to calm the fears of the isolationists in Congress, as the declaration was legally attached to the mandate of the League of Nations. Although it would still have been a stretch to argue that America, even de-facto, is part of the League by endorsing the Balfour Declaration, there were many in the Congress who wanted no ties to the organization, whether legally, or indirectly. In regards to the removal of "existing" from the text that was mainly deleted in order to pacify various Christian groups, as the deletion, it was asserted, would give guarantee that their status in the land was ironclad. Lastly, the omission of the "Jews in other countries", i.e. the Diaspora, was most likely expunged in order to mollify the Zionists, or even as a "reward" to them for their support in the House's deletion of the Balfour Declaration from the Congressional document.[329]

With the document now changed, the only difference between the House of Representative's proposal and that of the Senate's was that the House had a preamble to the text. This allowed for the Senate to move forward and indeed the resolution was brought forth for a vote. Senator Lodge, on May 3, 1922, secured a unanimous vote in the Senate in favor of the pro-Palestine Zionist resolution. Rabbi Glazer made the following remarks:

> The adoption of the resolution by the United States Senate ends the most glorious chapter in the history of the Jewish people in Diaspora. The fifteen million Jews the world over feel that the Anglo-Saxon civilization, both in England and the United States, is back on their long cherished hope to re-establish themselves as a nation not only to live independent and work out their own destiny, but to yield to the world once more

the spiritual fruit which has, since the days of the prophets, made this world worthwhile living in.[330]

Even though most work now appeared completed, there was still some wrangling in the House of Representatives over the House's proposed resolution. Throughout the month of May 1922, anti-Zionist pressure intensified throughout Washington, DC. The anti-Zionist block, which included the Reform movement, various Arab factions and State Department officials, were still dismayed with the phrase "*the* Jewish national home" instead of "*a* Jewish national home." Therefore, due to their pressure, the House Committee, on May 23, again changed the document to read "a Jewish national home", somewhat of a small blow to the Zionist movement, not to mention it must have irritated Congressman Fish and certainly Senator Lodge. The House Committee voted 10 to 2 in favor of the modification.[331] Regardless of the change, the House still supported the proposed Zionist idea.

During the month of May and up until a joint Congressional resolution would be introduced, many opponents of the resolution asked for the Congressional rationale for such support. Fish was more than willing to answer:

> This report expresses our moral interest in and our favorable attitude toward the establishment in Palestine of a national home for the Jewish people. It commits us to no foreign obligation or entanglements. The protection of the holy places is carefully provided for, as well as the right of Christian and all non-Jewish communities. There is a strong religious and humanitarian appeal in this recognition accorded to the Jewish people that goes beyond its purely material aspects...We of America should be glad to give our moral support to a project which is based on justice and humanity. To give this recognition to so laudable an endeavor of a people seeking to create a haven of refuge for the oppressed and homeless of their race is to act in consonance with the loftiest American ideals. The Jews have suffered greatly... The World War has overwhelmed them... They are seeking a home where with their generous help of their brethren of other lands who are in more comfortable circumstances, they may recreate their own forms of life, and realize their ideals...[332]

The Zionist movement, of course, was very pleased to hear such a pronouncement. However, many anti-Zionists immediately went on the offensive. At this point, although both Houses had not formally passed a joint resolution endorsing the creation of a Jewish national home, it appeared closer than ever. Yet the opponents of such a resolution believed that with enough pressure they might be able to stymie the whole process, slow it down, or at the very least make so many emendations to the text that it would have little to no prestige. The Reform movement, Arab factions, and *The New York Times* harshly attacked or condemned the Congress for seemingly taking a position on a "religious question." The Zionists, they stated, were "smuggling" in a proposal for the "Jewish religion" and that "such a motive has no place in American public councils…"[333]

Aside from any anti-Zionist lobbying throughout the month of May and then June, the House resolution was not altered. It would not be until the end of June, however, approximately one month after the final resolution was formed that the House of Representatives voted on the proposal. Without a recorded vote, and without any opposition being heard, House Joint Resolution 322 was passed on June 30, 1922.[334] Interestingly, on June 30 of that year, the House was schedule for a summer break, so to expedite the voting process they waived a debate and the resolution was passed without a single negative vote.[335]

Prior to the vote Congressman Fish reiterated several elements and reasons for supporting a pro-Zionist resolution. For one, he noted, Zionism was based on justice and humanity, and was presently trying to find a haven for battered Jews. Secondly, the resolution does not commit the United States to any foreign entanglement, nor does it require America to spend any money on the project, or if need arise, to support the Zionists militarily. Essentially, he summarized, the resolution was one of sympathy for the thousands of European Jews who needed a home of their own. In conclusion, Fish stated that the Jews should be able to recreate their culture on the land that God gave Abraham.

By July 1, 1922 both the Senate and the House of Representatives had endorsed a resolution very similar to the Balfour Declaration (the Senate on May 3, 1922, the House of Representatives on June 30, 1922). Yet there was still work to be done. Both Houses of Congress would still need to clarify any divergent language in the text, issue a joint Senate-House resolution, see to it that it passes, and then approach the President of the United States for his endorsement and signature. Simultaneously, the Zionist movement, along with Lodge and Fish, would have to quell any opposition to the resolutions while gathering support from needed White House officials.

From The State Department
To The White House

Following the May and June 1922 passing of a pro-Zionist resolution in both the Senate and House – though it was not yet a joint resolution – many anti-Zionists went on the offensive. Although it has already been shown that numerous Arab and Jewish opponents of Zionism pleaded in and out of the Congress in order to influence members not to support a pro-Zionist resolution, there were others who, for various reasons, also lobbied against any American declaration. The most vocal and overt opponent of Zionism in America, aside from several Jewish and Arab groups, was the Department of State. The history and relationship between the State Department and Zionism has been well documented.[336] However, during the crucial months leading up to the joint Congressional resolution, State had increased its voice of opposition.

Subsequent to the Balfour Declaration, which created an aura of prestige for the Zionist movement, the State Department began to take Zionism more seriously, and in most cases with caution. Although President Wilson openly stated his approval of the Balfour Declaration, his cabinet advisors and members of the State Department felt he was too hasty in lending his voice to the pronouncement. The Secretary of State, Robert Lansing, made known his discomfort and disappointment in Wilson for not adequately consulting him before the President made his remarks regarding Balfour.[337]

Three of Lansing's main concerns, aside from not being consulted – he was, after all, the Secretary of State and the Balfour Declaration was an international statement – was that he felt that the US should stay out of potential foreign entanglements, regardless of the fact that America was officially at war. However, as noted earlier, America was not at war with Turkey, and Lansing saw no need to antagonize or even potentially open up another war front.[338] Secondly, the Secretary of State openly stated that the Jews themselves were not united on the Zionist cause.[339] Lastly, Lansing did not want to upset those Christian denominations who would have felt affronted by the Holy Land being back in the hands of the "Christ killers."[340] As many others have pointed out, the subsequent decade in particular and the ensuing ones in general would see many more individuals who harbored such attitudes towards Zionism and the Jews. The consequence was that the Executive Office of the President and the Department of State literally attempted to execute varying policies in regards to Zionism.[341]

However, somewhat absent from the public debate was the State Department's position regarding the use of crude oil for the American military, a significant component to understanding their position. An alliance with the Zionists, many in State felt, ran the risk of America being cut off from Middle Eastern oil supplies. Throughout World War I and subsequent to it, the United States, as well as Britain, was sensitive to this potential dilemma. With the American oil supply depleted by War's end, new outlets were needed, and the most talked about reserves were the Arabian Desert.[342] Indeed, by the time the Paris Peace Conference of 1919 had been called for, oil, it appears, was a factor that would dictate, or at the very least play a role, in American policy at the meetings.[343]

By 1920 and as the Zionist movement was crumbling, the State Department would offer another reason for denouncing the goals of Zionism. The charge that Zionism was a "Socialist Movement," department officials maintained, should be enough for any American administration to distance itself from it, if not abandon the project altogether. This position was maintained by State Department officials for years to come, and appears to have been brought to the Department by Consular George Cobb in a report from Jerusalem. On May 5, 1920 Cobb separated the Socialist Zionists into three groups.[344]

International Social Zionists. They were described as "intellectual socialists who wish to use their racial connections to promote Socialist organization."

Bolshevist Zionists. They were described as "ultra radicals who find it impossible to pursue their ends within the other groups."

Palestinian Zionists. This group was described as socialists of "old Spanish-Jewish (Sephardic) origin, more familiar with Arabic, good Hebrew, and the ways of the orient."

Although some in the State Department believed that America should "watch out" for these Jewish socialists, for the most part, however, this factor did not contribute to the overall position of State in regards to Zionism. The oil factor was considered more pressing.

Yet by 1922, during the Congressional hearings on Zionism, the noted negative factors concerning Zionism held little sway over Senator Lodge, Senator Curtis, and Congressman Fish. Certainly many leaders, Lodge in particular, had believed that Jewish settlement in Palestine would be beneficial to American interests in the region by having the Jews engage in commerce. Lodge, of course, was an isolationist, but it can be argued that he was an isolationist in terms of getting the US involved in Europe (or re-involved in Europe), and not the Middle East or Palestine. In regards to other factors that swayed Lodge, Curtis and Fish, as well as some State Department officials that Zionism was in the best interest of the country, was both the missionaries and the oil work being undertaken in Palestine.

Missionaries, who had been present in Palestine prior to the turn of the 20th Century, had convinced many Arabs that American involvement in the region should be embraced. The missionaries brought a message of peace and were generally, at first, trusted by the Arabs. Furthermore, oil interests in Palestine were still in its infant stages of development, and certainly companies that had a stake in the petroleum market there leaned on government officials in America to do all in their power to secure the continuance of their work. These and other factors played a prominent role in many Congressional members support for a pro-Zionist resolution, thus leading many members of Congress to ignore any of the negative reports about Zionism.

However, following the passing of the Palestine resolutions in both Houses of Congress, the Department of State was put in a quagmire. After all, their main concern was American involvement overseas, and department officials believed that neither Zionism (nor Arab nationalism) mattered much for America. Thus it was maintained that American neutrality abroad would be compromised by any American support for the goals of Zionism, whether in statement or deed. Therefore, even after the Congress approved the Lodge and Fish resolutions, and, as will be shown, after President Harding signed the joint resolution, the State Department maintained that America had no authority to implement the Balfour Declaration, or had any say in the administration of the Palestine Mandate.[345] This was strictly a British decision.

Even though Secretary of State Hughes studied the various pro-Palestine drafts with Senator Lodge he ultimately disapproved of its content.[346] Hughes, however, had been antagonistic of Zionist aims for quite some time by the time Lodge approached him.[347] He and others were disappointed when the resolution passed, even though it "committed us (America) to no foreign obligations or entanglements." Regardless, the State Department maintained that the resolution implied American involvement overseas.[348] Secretary Hughes' top man on the Near East Desk, Allen Dulles, who would play a prominent role in the next several decades as being one of the most vocal antagonists of Zionism (Allen Dulles later became head of the CIA; his brother John Foster Dulles became Secretary of State) noted to the President and members of Congress not to get involved in the Middle East. However, to his consternation, he was ignored.[349]

Zionist officials knew very well the ambivalence of the State Department's position on Zionism, and often the leaders of the movement warned their colleagues regarding their view. Chain Weizmann, too, was weary of the Eastern Desk's opposition and often labeled their actions as "hostile".[350] However, even though State Department officials gave a tepid response, it was not only due to anti-Jewish sentiment or to American isolationism following World War I. Economic factors, such as oil and trade, as noted above, played a role in their outright rejection of American support. However, coupled with their ambivalent stance against Zionism along with the economic factor, State Department officials' negative sentiments towards Zionism were certainly amplified.[351]

Allen Dulles helped set this tone. He would not, however, publicly state that his negative view of Jews played a role in his opposition to Zionism. In fact, he wrote (in an internal division memo) that American interests in the region should be the only goal of his department.[352] Specifically, he listed missionary activity and American trade in the region and treaty rights that had been present for decades as the prime importance. In addition, in regards to American entanglement overseas, Zionism, to Dulles, was a British issue and one that had to do with the Versailles Treaty.[353]

In other memos circling throughout the State Department would be a well cited document that attempted to exonerate Dulles from all charges of anti-Semitism. In a brief against Zionism, several items were listed that "made sense" as to why America should not support the movement. Some of the forthcoming information is listed above; however a more concise list is as follows:

- Zionism does not "fit" the traditional American interest in the region.

- Even though America was in the throes of negotiations with France and England in order to secure its rights in the Middle East there was little reason for the United States to complicate matters more by adding new difficulties to the process.
- The American foreign policy sentiment post World War I was one of isolation.
- Lastly, the Jewish position in Palestine reached around 10%, while the other 90% vehemently opposed Zionism.[354]

Although the State Department harbored these views and certainly influenced many, their voice of opposition mattered little for Senator Lodge, Senator Curtis, and Congressman Fish. Despite the State Department's objections, and notwithstanding both Arab and some Jewish pressure not to lend their support to the Zionist initiative, the Senate and the House of Representatives, i.e. the entirety of the American Congress, each passed a separate resolution supporting Zionism. During the summer months the Zionist movement went on the offensive by lobbying government officials as well as ordinary citizen by publishing editorials and articles on the merits of Zionism. The movement even employed the Society of Friends of a Jewish Palestine, a Christian group, as noted earlier, that sought to lobby both at the grassroots and at the government level.[355]

By mid-Summer 1922 two important components remained to be undertaken: a joint Senate-House resolution and the President's signature. On July 12, 1922 the Senate submitted to the law body a resolution without a preamble, (in contradistinction from the May 3, 1922 that had one). The deletion of the preamble would make various parties, such as the State Department, non-Zionists and isolationists more content (or less nervous).[356] On the same day, without a record vote and without debate, the resolution passed.[357] The last hurdle before it could get to the President's desk was for the House of Representatives to strike out the preamble and vote on the resolution. On September 11, 1922, on a motion by Congressman Fish, the House of Representatives voted to delete the preamble. Thus Resolution 322 became "Joint Resolution 322," where both Houses of Congress now officially supported the creation of a Jewish national home in Palestine.[358] Shortly after the September 11 vote even the State Department hesitantly gave its consent to the President for his endorsement.[359] Joint Resolution 322 read as follows:

Be it resolved by the United States Senate and House of Representatives that the United States of America favors the establishment in Palestine of the national homeland for the Jewish people, in accordance with the provisions contained in the Declaration of the British Government of November 2, 1917, known as the Balfour Declaration, it being clearly understood that nothing shall be done which may prejudice the civil and religious rights of non-Jewish communities in Palestine, or the rights and political status enjoyed by Jews in any other country, and that the holy places and religious buildings and sites in Palestine shall be adequately protected.

> *Palestine Lodge-Fish Resolution*
> *September 11, 1922.*[360]

Ten days later, on September 22, 1922, President Harding, who verbally agreed that he would sign the resolution if both Houses of Congress endorsed it, signed the *Palestine Lodge-Fish Resolution*, thus beginning the official American involvement in Zionist (and later Israeli) affairs.

In Retrospect

The adoption of the Palestine Lodge-Fish Resolution was a monumental achievement for Simon Glazer, the Zionist Organization of America, and the World Zionist Organization, under Chaim Weizmann, who commissioned Glazer to undertake the project. Emotions ran high among the various Zionists groups and many were fearful that the United States would not support the endeavor. Had the US not leant its support the Zionists would have considered this a grave defeat. By early May 1922 though, it appeared that this was not to be the case.[361]

Following the passage in early September of the joint Congressional Resolution, several political figures, including some Jews, downplayed its significance. The arguments put forth were that the Resolution had "no force in law" and was "merely an expression of sympathy." This idea, according to some, was the interpretation of the State Department.[362] Regardless of the criticism by those who wanted to spoil the mood, the lasting contribution of the Resolution, signed by the President, has resonated until this very day. Zionism was given formal approval by the United States government, the first such time in American history. For Glazer, Zionism and the United States were linked by destiny.[363]

Within days of the President's endorsement of the Palestine Resolution, letters of gratitude and commendation poured into Glazer's office.[364] Letters from Jewish leaders, Senators, and friends could be seen in Glazer's Kansas City office well into 1923.[365] By the middle of September 1922, Glazer had written a short pamphlet explaining the actions he undertook in his quest for the passing of the Resolution. A good part of Glazer's pamphlet was referenced for this work.[366] After the Lodge-Fish Resolution was adopted, however, Glazer played a less prominent role in Zionist affairs. On occasion he did continue to meet with politicians and write letters on behalf of Zionism to those he believed could assist the movement.[367]

One of most significant reasons why Glazer continuously worked on behalf of Zionism was for the interest of the Jewish refugees in Europe. He wanted the United States to exert enough pressure on England that it forced the gates of Palestine open to Jewish immigration. For this purpose, in later years Glazer called upon Senator Curtis many times for guidance and access to President Calvin Coolidge, the Vice President under Harding who succeeded him as President. On October 24, 1923

Curtis arranged a meeting between Glazer and the new President. The Senator even went so far as to write another recommendation on behalf of Glazer.[368] Two days later, Glazer himself wrote a letter to the President. As a prelude to their meeting, Glazer wanted to make several points clear.

Firstly, he reminded Coolidge that Harding had supported Zionism. Additionally, Congress had passed two resolutions supporting the creation of a Jewish national home in Palestine. Therefore, it clearly was American policy that Zionist goals be achieved.[369] Glazer also informed Coolidge "For reasons unknown to us, (the gates of Palestine) still remain closed to Jewish immigration."[370] Before his meeting with the President, Glazer wrote that he wanted Coolidge to know that he would be asking him to do all he could to open the gates of Palestine for Jews to enter.[371]

Glazer did meet with Coolidge and noted that the President "took the suggestion very favorably and that he expressed his willingness to take up the matter with the State Department."[372] In fact, on October 29, 1923, Glazer received a letter from Senator Curtis explaining to him that he (and the administration) had already taken the matter up with State.[373] Of course, though, the State Department did not want to get the United States involved in foreign affairs.[374] Glazer replied to the White House on November 22 clarifying his remarks. He wanted the administration to understand that by opening the gates of Palestine, the "immigration problem here (in the US) could be relieved."[375] The President's secretary wrote back two days later and said "this matter is properly for the consideration of the State Department."[376]

Three weeks later, Glazer again wrote the White House, imploring the Secretary of the President to let Coolidge know that he was not affiliated with any organization except the Central Conference of Orthodox Rabbis of America and Canada, which he led. The reasons for Glazer's consistent pursuit of the President on behalf of Zionism, he wrote, strictly came from his religious and humanitarian side.[377] He also wrote that he had the highest respect and admiration for Coolidge. Writing to Slemp (the President's secretary/chief of staff) on October 28, he said, "I believe that he has something great within himself which is bound to appear sooner or later, so that his countrymen may know and appreciate him." Glazer asked Slemp to express these sentiments to the President.[378] Although Slemp beseeched the President (and many intervened with future Presidents) nothing happened with regard to Jewish immigration to Palestine. As history has shown, rather bitterly, the gates of the land of Israel were shut to the Jews, even in throes of the systematic genocide of European Jewry during World War II. It would not be until May 14, 1948, when the British Mandate ended and the Jews proclaimed national independence in their ancient homeland that the gates of Israel were freely opened.

There were many key players, both Jew and non-Jew, who actively participated in the creation of a Jewish national home in the early 1920s and more particularly, helped influence the American position regarding Zionism. On American shores, two non-Jewish men stand out head and shoulders above many in their support for Zionism, Senator Charles Curtis and Senator Henry Cabot Lodge. Curtis's career in the Senate, over twelve years, helped pave the way for men like Glazer to reach powerful individuals such as the President and Secretary of State. Curtis's influence and friendship with the American Jewish community reached its climax in the late 1920s when many Jews wanted him to run for President. Glazer would have liked nothing more than to see his old friend and colleague win the Presidency, but he would not allow himself to endorse Curtis. Glazer, as noted earlier, was not affiliated with any political organization except for the Central Council of Orthodox Rabbis of America and Canada.[379]

Curtis also fought for many Jewish rights, aside from Zionism. The same year that Curtis was considering running for President, he was petitioned by Glazer to help alleviate the financial burden of Jews during the Passover season. For many years, American Jews imported *Matzo* (unleavened bread on the holiday of Passover) from overseas. Tariffs were high and Jewish shop owners had been raising prices for years. Glazer asked Curtis to intervene and speak with the head of the Tariff Commission with the intent to place Matzo on the "Free List," thus saving thousands of dollars of what appeared to be unfair tariffs.[380] Curtis arranged a meeting between Glazer and Thomas O. Marvin, the Chairman of the US Tariff Commission. He explained the situation and Marvin agreed wholeheartedly. No specific time line was given, but Glazer stated that the tariffs were eventually abolished.[381]

For many years, Curtis had been a staunch ally of the American Jewish community. In recognition of this fact, the Central Council of Orthodox Rabbis of America and Canada unanimously adopted a resolution on January 5, 1932, proclaiming that the members of the organization were buying 10,000 dunams of land in Palestine to be named "Curtishiah", the "City of Salvation," after Charles Curtis. The location would either be in the Mt. Carmel region, or in the vicinity of Jerusalem. Day and night, the council claimed, twenty men would always be studying Torah in the *Beth Hamidrash* (study house) of Curtishiah.[382] Upon reading the letter from Glazer, Curtis was deeply moved, yet had reservations.[383] However, when Curtis's reservations were put to rest, he gave his approval for the project to commence.[384] Glazer's friendship with Curtis lasted for many years until the Senator/ Vice President's death in 1934.

Curtis's Senate colleague, Henry Cabot Lodge, known as a staunch isolationist, supported the Zionist cause for a number of reasons, as did Congressman Hamilton Fish. All three men did not subscribe to the State Department's notion that a Jewish enclave or state in Palestine entangled the US in foreign affairs. They asserted that Palestinian Jewry would be an ally of America. Some of their Christian sentiments played a part in their support for Zionism as well.

Zionist leaders like Glazer and Weizmann played a major role in swaying politicians and government officials to support Zionism. Earlier historians credited much of the success of the Resolution to the efforts of Justice Louis Brandeis, American Jewry's leading Zionist advocate. My own research, however, indicates that although he played an important role in the Zionist movement he was not central to the dealings of the Lodge-Fish Resolution. Some claim that Brandeis should be given credit for the passage of the joint Congressional resolution due to his lobbying, although few historical documents back this up. The few historians who noted the Lodge-Fish Resolution in their writings gave Brandeis the majority of credit for the resolution's passage, although this may have been done inadvertently.[385] In all sources that I have analyzed, including primary material that was unavailable to earlier historians, Brandeis is simply not mentioned in any dealings in the Senate, the House of Representatives or the Executive Branch. The pivotal player in the unfolding events of the Palestine Lodge-Fish Resolution was Simon Glazer, who is also glaringly absent from previous historical research. Perhaps Glazer was forgotten – or more likely overlooked – because he was not part of the leadership of American Jewry or because he was not a political figure. Indeed, following the passage of the Resolution, Glazer essentially returned full time to the Rabbinate until his death, with occasional interventions with politicians when called upon. As for Brandeis, who at the time was synonymous with American Zionism, it was logical for many to attribute such a success to him. After all, his prominence of being a Supreme Court Justice would have given him access to the top politicians in the country. If Brandeis was part of the Lodge-Fish Resolution process it was not evident in my sources. Future historians may uncover new sources indicating that he played a role, but for the moment I have to revise the common view that Brandeis was key to the passage of the Resolution.

My concern in this work has been on the process that produced the Palestine Lodge-Fish Resolution. What was the impact of America's Balfour Declaration? I would argue that the Palestine Lodge-Fish Resolution appears to be the most significant political achievement of the Zionist movement since the passage of the actual Balfour Declaration five years prior, and indeed it is the most significant document in American Zionist history until 1948. The Resolution set in motion the relationship of the American government with Zionism – and by extension the longstanding American-Israeli relationship – for nearly a century. Thus, if the Resolution was so significant why have so few heard about it, and why has no one written any extensive piece on it until now?

There are essentially five major reasons that overshadowed the Resolution's impact. The first was the distaste for US intervention overseas following World War I. Isolationism had swept across the United States. Even a resolution that called for foreign intervention while offering only symbolic support (and even if no resources were to be allocated) was politically untenable. The second factor was the stock market crash of 1929 and the Great Depression that ensued. Foreign issues, especially ones not related to the economic crisis receded in importance. Job creation and economic revival were paramount. Third, it was Great Britain that controlled the Mandate on Palestine, not the United States. While the US could have urged Great Britain to expedite the Balfour Declaration, no American administration, nor Congress, could force this acceleration. Encouraging Britain cost little, but tangible actions on the ground were not realistic.

The fourth factor that led to the overshadowing of the Palestine Lodge-Fish Resolution was the onset of Second World War. In 1939, with Europe facing a Nazi onslaught, and then in late 1941 with the US involvement in the War, no meaningful action was to take place vis-à-vis Zionism. Prior to the War's commencement, in 1939 England slapped the Zionist movement with its infamous "White Paper", which limited Jewish immigration to Palestine to 75,000 through 1945. This White Paper has been viewed as a death sentence for European Jewry. Even in the throes of the mass extermination of European Jewry,

England did not budge from its quotas, and indeed fewer than 75,000 Jews, less than the quota allowed, immigrated to Palestine between 1939 and 1945.

The fifth factor that overshadowed the Resolution, which is tied to the fourth, was the *Shoah*, or Catastrophe, of European Jewry, also known as the Holocaust. So tremendous was the loss of life that any discussion of previous arrangements between the Zionists and Great Britain was given urgent attention, namely the Balfour Declaration. Indeed in 1944, prior the War's ending, members of the US Congress, acutely aware of the European Jewry's demise, invoked the Palestine Lodge-Fish Resolution in their attempt to convince Great Britain to implement the Balfour Declaration.[386] Following WWII, the US took on a more proactive role lobbying the British to open the gates of Palestine to Jewish refugees. By 1947 England handed the Palestine Mandate over to the newly formed United Nations, which on November 29, 1947 approved the creation of a Jewish state. England was to leave Palestine in May of the following year. Thus, the Palestine Lodge-Fish Resolution became lost to history, as did Rabbi Glazer and his efforts. The immediate impact of the Resolution was subtle. However, the Resolution had an indirect, long-term impact, and indeed the United States and the State of Israel are today close allies, sharing many bonds of commonality that stretch back to 1922. Many ordinary citizens and leading politicians agreed with Rabbi Glazer's view of Zionism and Americanism and the mutual benefit that would be achieved with the creation of a home for the Jews on their ancient soil. Glazer wrote:

> Their ambition to establish themselves as a nation is not only to live independent and work out their own destiny, but to yield to the world once more the spiritual fruit which has, since the days of the prophets, made this world worth living in.[387]

Even though the Palestine Lodge-Fish Resolution was forgotten by history, it is still important because it set the wheels in motion for the long and prosperous relationship between the United States and Zionism. The Resolution paved the way for Zionism to become part of the discourse of American politics, inside both Houses of Congress and inside the Executive branch even until today.

Bibliography

Archival

"Anches Interview," folder, Washington State Jewish Historical Society (WSJHS) Archive, University of Washington, November 24, 1981, Seattle, Washington.

Buttnick, Meta. "Congregation Bikkur-Cholim-Machzikay Hadath of Seattle: The Beginning years," *Western States Jewish History, Vol. 22*, 1915-1925.

League of Nations, Mandate for Palestine, Command #1785, Article 6, 1922.

Louis Lipsky Papers, Box 1920-1922, American Jewish Historical Society, P- 672., New York, NY.

Papers Relating to the Foreign Relations of the United States: The Lansing Papers 1914-1925 (Washington, D.C.: Government Printing Office, 1935-1940).

President Harding Papers, Ohio Historical Society in Marion, Ohio, 1921-1923, Box Titled "1922".

The Massachusetts Resolution is printed in the *Congressional Record*, vol. 62, part 5, p. 4,758.

Yeshiva University Archives, records of the Central Relief Committee, 198/8.

Simon Glazer Papers. Box 269, American Jewish Archives, Cincinnati, OH, 1938, all boxes.

Journals And Periodicals

Adler, Selig. "The Palestine Question in the Wilson Era," in *Jewish Social Studies* 10 (1948).

"American Rights in Palestine" in *The Nation* (July 12, 1922), pp. 22-46.

Assembly Herald, vol. 24 (Feb. 1918), p. 106; *Lutheran Companion*, vol. 26 (March 16, 1918), p. 130.

Berlin, George L. "The Brandeis-Weizmann Dispute," in *American Jewish Historical Quarterly* 60 (1970-1971): p. 37, 40.

Buttnick, Meta. "Congregation Bikkur-Cholim-Machzikay Hadath of Seattle: The Beginning Years," *Western States Jewish History, Vol. 22*, 1915-1925.

Central Conference of American Rabbis Year Book, vol. 27 (Philadelphia: Jewish Publication Society of America), p. 132.

Christian Century, vol. 39 (July 13, 1922), pp. 873-875.

Clay, Albert T. "Political Zionism," in *Atlantic Monthly*, vol. CXXVII (Feb., 1921), pp. 268-69.

Colby, Bainbridge. "The United States of America and the British Mandates," in *Contemporary Review* (Feb. 1921).

Continent, vol. L (July 29, 1920), p. 975.

Cohen, Morris R. "Zionism: Tribalism or Liberalism?" in the *New Republic*, vol. XIV (March 2, 1918), pp. 141-42.

Cook, Harold R. "William Eugene Blackstone," in *The New International Dictionary of the Christian Church* ed. J.D. Douglas (Exeter, Paternoster, 1974), p. 134.

Earl, Edward Meade. "Oil and American Foreign Policy," in the *New Republic* (Aug. 20, 1924).

Friedman, Isaiah, "Efraim and Inari Karsh, Empires of the Sand: The Struggle For Mastery in the Middle East, 1789-1923" in *Israel Studies* Volume 7, Number 1 (Spring 2002), pp. 222-230.

Goldblatt, Israel. "The Impact of the Balfour Declaration in America," in *American Jewish Historical Quarterly* (1967-1968) #57, pp. 457-458.

Hadassah Magazine, March 2002, Vol. 83 No. 7 p. 2.

Hoffman, Joshua, "Rav Kook's Mission to America" in *Orot* Vol. 1 (1991).

Kohler, Max J. "Some Early American Zionist Projects," in *Publications of the American Jewish Historical Society*, vol. # 8 (New York, NY, 1900), p. 75.

Kosofsky, Scott Martin. *From Boston Jews and American Zionism*, Yale University Press, 2005.

Mahoney, John F. "About this Issue" in *The Link (Americans for Middle East Understanding)* Vol. 25, No. 4 October/November 1992, p. 2.

Mandel, Neville. "Turks, Arabs and Jewish Immigration into Palestine, 1882-1914," in *St. Anthony's Papers*, no. 17, *Middle Eastern Affairs* (Oxford: 1965), pp. 77-108.

North American Review, vol. CCXVII (Jan. 1923), pp. 84-95.

Sherman, C. Bezalel. "Nationalism, Secularism, and Religion

in the Jewish Labor Movement," in *Judaism*, vol. 3 (Fall, 1954), p. 355.

Survey, vol. XLI (Dec. 28, 1918), pp. 391-393.

The Month, vol. CXXXVI (Sep. 1920), pp. 168-69, 268.

Wentling, Sonja. "Hoover, Palestine, and American Jews" in *American Jewish Archives* Vol. 53 (2001).

Secondary Sources

Adler, Cyrus, and Aaron Margalith. *With Firmness in the Right: American Diplomatic Action Affecting Jews 1840-1945* (New York: AJC, 1946).

Baram, Philip J. The *Department of State in the Middle East 1919-1945* (Philadelphia: University of Pennsylvania Press, 1978), p. 53.

Barker, Ray Sannard. *Woodrow Wilson and World Settlement* vol. II (Gloucester, MA: Doubleday, 1960 - first published in 1922-), vol. II, pp. 205- 219.

Barnard, Harry. *The Forging of an American Jew: The Life and Times of Judge Julian W. Mack* (New York: Herzl Press, 1974), p. 281.

Brecher, Frank W. *Reluctant Ally: United States Foreign Policy Towards the Jews from Wilson to Roosevelt* (New York: Greenwood Press, 1991).

Cohen, Naomi W. *The Year After the Riots: American Responses to the Palestine Riots of 1929-39* (Detroit: Wayne State Univ, 1988).

Crawley, Peter. *A Descriptive Bibliography of the Mormon Church. Volume One, 1830-1847* (Utah: Brigham Young University, Religious Studies Center, 1997), esp. pp. 187-89.

Curry, R., and Brown, T. *Conspiracy: The Fear of Subversion in American History* (New York: Holt, Rinehart and Winston, 1972), p. 145.

Davis, Moshe. *With Eyes Toward Zion: Scholars Colloquium on America-Holy Land Studies* (New York: Arno, 1977), p. 19.

Encyclopedia Judaica (Jerusalem: Keter Publishing House Jerusalem Ltd., 1972).

Fausold, Martin L. *The Presidency of Herbert C. Hoover Life* (New York: Knopf, 1979).

Fink, Reuben. *America and Palestine* (New York, American Zionist Emergency Council, 1945), pp. 20-22.

Finkelstein, Louis. *Jewish Self-Government in the Middle Ages*, (Westport, CT: Greenwood Press, 1972).

Flohr, Paul Mendes, and Reinharz, Jehuda. *The Jew in the Modern World* (Oxford and New York, Oxford University Press, 1980), pp. 377-87.

Friedman, Isaiah. *Germany, Turkey, and Zionism, 1897-1918* (Oxford, Clarendon, 1977).

Glazer, Simon. *Guide of Judaism: A Systematic Work for the Study and Instruction of the Whole Scope of Judaism* (New York, 1925).

Glazer, Simon. *The Jews of Iowa* (Des Moines: Koch Bros. Printing Co. 1904), Chapter 21, p. 1.

Glazer, Simon. *The Palestine Resolution* (Kansas City, Mo., 1922),

Goldhagen, Daniel Jonah. *Hitler's Willing Executioners* (New York, 1996), p. 49.

Haas, Jacob. *Louis D. Brandeis: A Biographical Sketch* (New York, 1929, p. 81.

Halpern, Ben. *The Idea of the Jewish State* (London, 1970).

Hertzberg, Arthur. *The Jews in America: Four Centuries of an Uneasy Encounter: A History* (New York: Simon & Schuster, 1989), pp. 222-25.

Herztberg, Arthur. *The Zionist Idea* (Cleveland and New York The World Publishing Company and Jewish publication Society of America, 1959), pp. 331-350.

Homer, E. *Arthur Capper, Publisher, Politician, and Philanthropist* (Lawrence: University of Kansas Press, 1962), Introduction.

Hyde, Orson. *A Voice from Jerusalem* (Liverpool: James and Woodburn, 1842).

Kaplan, Robert. *The Arabists: The Romance of an American Elite* (New York, The Free Press, 1993), p. 49.

Kelly, J. N. D. *Early Christian Doctrine* (San Francisco, Harper & Row, 1978), p. 190.

Khalidi, Rashid. *British Policy towards Syria and Palestine 1906-1914: A Study of the Antecedents of the Hussein-McMahon Correspondence, the Sykes-Picot Agreement and the Balfour Declaration* (London, Ithaca Press, 1980).

Klieman, Aaron. *Zionist Political Activity in the 1920's and 1930's* (New York: Garland Publishing, 1987).

Kook, Abraham Isaac R. *Iggerot Rayah* (Mossad Harav Kook: Jerusalem, 1965).

Laqueur, Walter. *History of Zionism* (New York: Schocken,1989), p. 270.

Lederhendler, Eli and Sarna, Jonathan. *America and Zion: Essays and Papers in Memory of Moshe Davis*, (Wayne State University Press: Detroit, 2002), pp. 49-73.

Lewis, Bernard, *The Shaping of the Modern Middle East* (New York and Oxford: Oxford University Press, 1994), pp. 71-163.

Lindbert, Berth. *A God-Filled Life: The Story of W. E. Blackstone* (American Missionary Society, 1987).

Link, Arthur S. *The Papers of Woodrow Wilson* (Princeton: Princeton University Press, 1986), 55, pp. 438-39.

Lipsky, Louis. *Thirty Years of American Zionism* vol. I (New York, 1927), pp. 65-72.

Macnulty, W. Kirk. *Freemasonry: A Journey Through Ritual and Symbol, Art & Imagination* (New York: Thames & Hudson, September 1991).

Manuel, Frank E. *The Realities of American-Palestine Relations* (Washington DC: Public Affairs Press, 1949), p. 172.

Margolis, Max and Marx, Alexander, *A History of the Jewish People* (Philadelphia, Jewish Publication Society of America, 1947).

Meinertzhagen, Richard. *Middle East Diary 1917-1956* (London, 1959), pp. 55-56.

Merkley, P. C. *The Politics of Christian Zionism 1891-1948* (London: Frank Cass, 1998), p. 14.

Meyer, Isidore S. *Early History of Zionism in America* (New York: American Jewish Historical Soc. and Herzl Press, 1958), pp. 1-20.

Miller, David Hunter. *My Diary at the Conference of Paris: Policy towards Palestine*, vol. 4 (New York, 1924), pp. 263-64.

Minerbi, Sergio. *The Vatican and Zionism* (New York: Oxford University Press, 1990).

Morgenthau, Henry. *All in a Lifetime* (Garden City, NY: 1922), p. 104.

Murray, Robert K. *The Harding Era* (Minn: University of Minnesota Press, 1969).

Parkes, James, *The Conflict of the Church and the Synagogue: A Study in the Origins of Antisemitism* (New York: Athenuem, 1969), pp. 163-166.

Rausch, David A. *Zionism within early American Fundamentalism, 1878-1918: A Convergence of Two Traditions* (New York: Mellen Press, 1979).

Richardson, James D. *A Compilation of the Messages and Papers of the Presidents,* 11 vols. (Washington: Government Printing House, 1817-1898), p. 188.

Richter, Julius. *A History of Protestant Missions in the Near East* (New York: AMS Press, 1970).

Rose, Norman. *Chaim Weizmann: A Biography* (New York: Viking Press, 1986), p. 210.

Safran, Nadav. *The United States and Israel* (Cambridge: Harvard University Press, 1963), p. 36.

Schama, Simon. *Two Rothchilds and the Land of Israel* (New York: Alfred A. Knopf, 1978), p. 168.

Schult, P. *Mid-America's Promise: A Profile of Kansas City Jewry* (Kansas City, 1982).

Shalom, Ish. *Rav Avraham Itzhak HaCohen Kook: Between Rationalism and Mysticism* (New York: State University of New York Press, 1993), pp. 11-15.

Shapiro, Yonathan. *The Formative Years of the Israeli Labour Party: The Organization of Power 1919-1930* (London: Sage Publications, 1976), p. 73.

Sharif, Regina. *Non-Jewish Zionism, Its Roots in Western History* (London: Zed Pub., 1983).

Sherman, Moshe D. *Orthodox Judaism in America: A Biographical Dictionary and Sourcebook* (Connecticut and London: Greenwood Press, 1996), p. 76.

Shuman, Bernard. *A History of the Sioux Jewish Community: 1869-1969* (Iowa: Jewish Federation of Sioux City, 1969), Introduction.

Stein, Leonard. *The Balfour Declaration* (London, Vallentine, Mitchell, 1961).

Stoyanovsky, J. *The Mandate for Palestine* (London, New York, Toronto, 1928), pp. 66, 204-210.

Strum, Philippa, *Louis D. Brandeis: Justice for the People* (Cambridge, Mass.: Harvard University Press, 1984), pp. 256-266.

Syrkin, Marie, Syrkin, Nahman. *Socialist Zionist: A Biographical Memoir and Selected Essays* (New York: Herzl Press and Sharon Books, 1961), pp. 288-89.

Urofsky, Melvin. *American Zionism from Herzl to the Holocaust* (Lincoln, Nebraska and London: University of Nebraska Press), p. 113, 161-79;

Wagner, Donald E. *Anxious for Armageddon* (Scottsdale, Pennsylvania: Herald Press, 1995).

Walworth, Arthur. *Wilson and His Peacemakers: American Diplomacy at the Paris Peace Conference, 1919* (Norton & Co: New York & London, 1986), pp. 479-481.

Wasserstein, Bernard. *The Letters and Papers of Chaim Weizmann Vol. X, July 1920 - December 1921* (Transaction Books, Rutgers University, Israel University Press, Jerusalem, 1977), p. xii-xiii

Weisbord, R.G. *African Zion: The Attempt to Establish a Jewish Colony in the East African Protectorate 1903-1905* (Philadelphia: The Jewish Publication Society of America, 1968), pp. 1-33, 59-58.

Weizmann, Chaim. *Trial and Error* (New York: Harper, 1949), p. 200.

Zionist Organization of America, Brandeis on Zionism: A Collection of Addresses and Statements by Louis D. Brandeis (New York: H. Wolff, 1942), p. 29.

Newspapers

American Hebrew, New York, Nov. 16, 1917, Editorial.

American Israelite, New York, Aug. 1, 1919, p. 1.

Appeal, Memphis, Tenn., Dec. 1, 1918, Editorial.

Canadian Jewish Chronicle, May 9, 1924, p. 8

Courier, Waterloo, Iowa, Dec. 11, 1917, Editorial.

Continent, New York City, Dec. 27, 1917, Editorial.

Dayton News, Ohio, May 14, 1918, p. 2.

Der Forvertz (Forward), Nov. 24, 1917, Editorial.

Dos Diddishes Tageblatt, Nov. 8 and 18, 1917, Sept. 5, 1918.

Guardian, Patterson, New Jersey, Dec. 19, 1917 Editorial.

Kansas City Times, Kansas, May 18, 1918, p. 16.

Jewish Daily Bulletin, New York, Oct. 30, 1924, Editorial pp., 8-10.

Jewish Exponent, New York, Nov. 16, 1917, p. 22.

Morgen Journal Newspaper, April 16, 1924, p. 1-5.

New York Evening Globe, New York, Nov. 12, 1917, Editorial.

New York Herald, New York, April 14, 1917, Editorial.

The Boston Transcript, Massachusetts, December. 12, 1917, p. 3.

The Canadian Jewish Review, Vol. XXVI, February 11, 1944.

The Jewish Voice of the Pacific Coast
- April 26, 1918, p. 1.
- August 14, 1918, p. 1.

The New York Times
- March 3, 1919, p. 8.
- March 5, 1919, p. 12.
- Jan. 6, 1920, p. 7.
- Nov. 6 1922, p. 13.
- Numerous more citations to follow, pending further research.

Times, Denver, Colorado, May 8, 1918, p. 2.
Times of St. Louis, Missouri, Dec. 6, 1917, p. 12.

Websites

www.cjp.org/content_display.html?ArticleID=129998
www.csje.org
www.spartacus.schoolnet.co.uk/BUharmsworth.htm.
www.us-israel.org/jsource/Zionism.html.
www.wzo.org.il/en/resources/view.asp?id=1635.

Endnotes

1 "The Minutes of the Senate," September 11, 1922, Senate Archives, Washington, DC, 1922. President Harding signed the resolution on September 21, 1922. The American declaration, though similar to Britain's Balfour Declaration, was more detailed, particularly the last line, which specified that "holy places and religious buildings" were to be protected. This was not mentioned in the Balfour Declaration. The reason for inserting this sentence in the American version was to pacify Catholic and anti-Semitic Christian denominations in the United States. As will be shown, many Christians believed that the Jews would destroy the churches in the Holy Land if they took control of Palestine.

2 After World War I, the Allied Supreme Council determined to seek a solution for former Ottoman territories. The San Remo Conference, which took place in Italy from April 19-26, 1920, was specifically convened to allocate the Middle Eastern lands of the former Ottoman Empire. The decision of the conference reinforced the agreements signed at the London Conference of February 1920, including the Balfour Declaration of 1917. England, at San Remo, became the mandate holders of Palestine and Iraq, while France was designated the protector of Syria and (present- day) Lebanon.

3 This can be evidenced by the fact the a large majority of both Houses of Congress supported the forthcoming resolution on Palestine vis-à-vis a Jewish homeland. The joint resolution, and the Balfour Declaration before it, were viewed favorably by the U.S. Congress. For more on this see Paul C. Merkley, *The Politics of Christian Zionism 1891-1948* (United Kingdom: Routledge, 1998), p. 100.

4 For an elaboration of this idea, which included setting up American agricultural colonies throughout the United States to prepare for the second coming of Christ, as well as Christians converting to Judaism in order to hasten the redemption of the world, see Abraham J. Karp, "The Zionism of Warder Cresson," in *Early History of Zionism in America,* ed. Isidore S. Meyer (New York: American Jewish Historical Soc. and Herzl Press, 1958), pp. 1-20; Moshe Davis, "The Holy Land in American Spiritual History," in *With Eyes Toward Zion: Scholars Colloquium on America-Holy Land Studies,* ed. Moshe Davis (New York: Arno, 1977), p. 19.

5 Max J. Kohler, "Some Early American Zionist Projects," in
Publications of the American Jewish Historical Society, vol. # 8,
1900, p. 75; Michael J. Pragai, *Faith and Fulfillment: Christians and
the Return to the Promised Land* (London: Vallentine, Mitchell,
1985), p. 49. Much literature during the Colonial Period speaks
in terms of Manifest Destiny and the creation of a new "Israel,"
both in terms of people and land. In a more striking example
of this theme, an original design by Thomas Jefferson, Benjamin
Franklin and John Adams portrayed the Israelites crossing
the Red Sea with Pharaoh in pursuit. Moses is standing on the
other side of the sea. The axiom on the seal read: "Rebellion
to Tyrants is Obedience to God." This design, however, was
rejected.

6 Numerous works detail the origins and rationale of Christian
Messianic Zionism, including the evangelical and
fundamentalist approach. See, for instance, Regina Sharif, *Non-
Jewish Zionism, Its Roots in Western History* (London: Zed Pub.,
1983); Donald E. Wagner, *Anxious for Armageddon* (Scottsdale,
Pennsylvania: Herald Press, 1995); David A. Rausch, *Zionism
within early American Fundamentalism, 1878-1918: A Convergence
of Two Traditions* (New York: Mellen Press, 1979).

7 Christian sentiments regarding the land of Israel throughout
American history has been poignantly illustrated by John Davis,
who argues that by studying Holy Land paintings and maps
from 18th and 19th Century artists, a good portrayal of the love of
the average American for the land can be seen. See John Davis,
"Each Moldering ruin Recalls History: Nineteenth-Century
Images of Jerusalem and the American Public," in *America
and Zion: Essays and Papers in Memory of Moshe Davis*, ed. Eli
Lederhendler and Jonathan Sarna (Wayne State University
Press: Detroit, 2002), pp. 49-73.

8 Lincoln remarked that his chiropodist was a Jew who "has
so many times 'put me upon my feet' that I would have no
objection to giving his countrymen 'a leg up.'"

9 Although many Jews died from the pogrom, another characteristic
of the rampage was that approximately 20,000 Jews were
expelled from Moscow proper. Even though the majority of
pogroms ceased in 1884, over the course of the following ten
years tensions mounted. They climaxed, for the time being, in
1891, yet the press did all it could to add to the prevalent anti-
Semitism. Indeed, even the religious establishment added to
the tension. The head of the Holy Synod, the governing body of
the Orthodox Church, K. Pobedonostsey, lashed out at the Jews

as well, exclaiming the he desired that 1/3 of the Jews die, 1/3 convert to Christianity, while the remaining 1/3 leave Russia. It should be noted that both General Wallace and M.P. Oliphant continuously supported the Zionist cause, sometimes causing quite a commotion. See Regina Sharif, *Non-Jewish Zionism* (London: Zed Press, 1983), p. 68. See also Henry Butterfield Ryan *America's Jews and Russia's Tsars: The Struggle over Jewish Persecution, 1881-1917*, A Paper for the 2009 Conference of the Society of Historians of American Foreign Relations, pp. 1-13, and note 8.

10 Quoted in Reuben Fink's *America and Palestine* (New York, American Zionist Emergency Council, 1945), pp. 20-21.

11 Ibid., pp. 21-22.

12 The petition was to be sent to the following leaders and nations with the hope of garnering their support: Alexander III, Czar of Russia; Victoria, Queen of Great Britain and Empress of India; William II, Emperor of Germany; Francis Joseph, Emperor of Austro-Hungary; Abdul Hamid II, Sultan of Turkey; His Royal Majesty, Humbert, King of Italy; Her Royal Majesty Marie Christiana, Queen Regent of Spain; the Government of the Republic of France; Belgium, Holland, Denmark, Sweden, Portugal, Roumainia, Servia, Bulgaria and Greece.

13 For a history of Blackstone and his influential evangelical ideas, see Berth Lindbert, *A God-Filled Life: The Story of W. E. Blackstone* (American Missionary Society, 1987). It should be mentioned that in 1878 Blackstone wrote *Jesus is Coming,* a book which was republished in numerous editions during the following decades. Messianic expectations were widespread among evangelicals, particularly towards the end of the century. President Harrison, however, did not support the petition. It is interesting to note, however, that in 1965 Blackstone was honored in Jerusalem with memorial and a forest named after him. See Harold R. Cook, "William Eugene Blackstone," in *The New International Dictionary of the Christian Church,* ed. J.D. Douglas (Exeter, Paternoster, 1974), p. 134.

14 Although, of course, this was not always the case, as the Catholic Church and other Christian sects utterly rejected any doctrine that stated the Jews would return to the land of Israel. See, for instance, J. N. D. Kelly, *Early Christian Doctrine* (San Francisco, Harper & Row, 1978), p. 190. Justin Marty was explicit in that the Holy Land's possession had passed to the "New Israel". See Justin, Dialogue with Trypho, XI. In *Ante-Nicene Fathers*, vol. 1.

pp. 200-267. See also the writing of the 5th Century Christian theologian St. Augustine and St. John Chrysostom in James Parkes, *The Conflict of the Church and the Synagogue: A Study in the Origins of Antisemitism* (New York: Athenuem, 1969), pp. 163-166.

15 The Freemasons boasted a number of very influential figures, including Napoleon and George Washington. Each played prominent roles in their respective sectors (lodges). Freemasons claim their origins to the time of King Solomon, where they claim they played an active and dominant role in the building of the Temple in Jerusalem. Many claim that Freemasonry was created in Middle Ages, while others ascribe its creation to the year 1717 by a group of affluent Englishmen. The organization soon flourished, rapidly spreading throughout the British Empire. Masonic lodges appeared in the American colonies as early as the 1730s, while a similar strain later evolved in France and swept across Europe. President McKinley, (1897-1901) received his Capitular degrees in Canton, Ohio, in 1883 and was made a Knights Templar in 1884. The Knights Templar, it should be emphasized, claim they are the keepers of the Ark of the Covenant, or as they refer to it, "the treasure," among others spoils they claim to have acquired during the Crusades. There was also once a claim that Masons possessed the Ark. There is no doubt that many of these Mason and Templar legends played a significant role in the lives of the signatories of the Blackstone Memorial, as well as a role in the later support of Zionism by American government officials. It should added that of the subsequent six Presidents after McKinley, T. Roosevelt, W. Taft, W. Wilson, W. Harding, F.D. Roosevelt, and H. Truman, excluding Wilson, were all well-known Freemasons. President Harding, one of the key players of this Dissertation, was made a member of the Knights Templar in 1884 which may have played a role in his support for a Jewish national home, as messianic expectations were prevalent at that time. For an elaboration of Freemasonry, see W. Kirk Macnulty, *Freemasonry: A Journey Through Ritual and Symbol, Art & Imagination* (New York: Thames & Hudson, September 1991).

16 See, for instance, James D. Richardson, *A Compilation of the Messages and Papers of the Presidents,* 11 vols. (Washington: Government Printing House, 1817-1898), p. 188. Blackstone later sent the petition to (former) President Cleveland and then Roosevelt but nothing was done governmentally to support Zionism.

17 Aside from preaching, one of the missionaries' main occupations was that of a teacher, especially how to read and write. Now being able to read and write, many gave their love to the missionaries. See Robert Kaplan, *The Arabists: The Romance of an American Elite* (New York, The Free Press, 1993), p. 49. It should be noted that some maintain that once a significant educated class formed throughout the Near East, it helped create Arab Nationalism. See, for instance, Nadav Safran, *The United States and Israel* (Cambridge: Harvard University Press, 1963), p. 36.

18 It should be noted that Mormon missionaries, and more so Protestant missionaries, viewed their work in the Holy Land as being the purest form of Christian missionizing. Furthermore, in a sense, they were in the Holy Land to gather converts to usurp the power of the Catholic Church, who had "polluted" the land, they felt. On this see Julius Richter, *A History of Protestant Missions in the Near East* (New York: AMS Press, 1970); Steven Epperson, "Dedicating and Consecrating the Land: Mormon Ritual Performance in Palestine," in *America and Zion: Essays and Papers in Memory of Moshe Davis*, pp. 91-116. Although evangelical elements of the Mormon and mainstream Protestant branches of Christianity held views that the Jews would control the land of Israel prior to the second coming of Christ, the Catholic Church did not share these sentiments, and believed that if the Jews controlled the land, Christian churches would be threatened with destruction, and that missionary work would cease. On this see Sergio Minerbi, *The Vatican and Zionism* (New York: Oxford University Press, 1990).

19 The Church of Christ of Latter-day Saints, who are Mormon, sent at least six envoys to the Holy Land between the years 1841 and 1933 to "dedicate and consecrate" the land for the ingathering of the Jewish exiles and the beginning of Jewish political autonomy. For some early primary material on Mormonism and its view of the Jews and Palestine, see Orson Hyde, *A Voice from Jerusalem* (Liverpool: James and Woodburn, 1842). For a more on the modern day Mormon approach to early Latter-day Saints' ideas of Jewish political autonomy, which includes the ingathering of the exiles, see Peter Crawley, *A Descriptive Bibliography of the Mormon Church. Volume One, 1830-1847* (Utah: Brigham Young University, Religious Studies Center, 1997), esp. pp. 187-89.

20 The term "rapture" comes from the Latin verb *raptare*, and the Greek word *harpizo*, both meaning "to be caught up" or "to be grabbed/snatched up", as Jesus will "take" his people to

heaven before the destruction transpires. The rapture, and those "born again" Christians who will be taken to heaven prior to the arrival of Jesus, is said to originate from a literal understanding of 1 Thessalonians 4:16, in the New Testament.

21 For an elaboration of the Rapture, see John F. Mahoney, "About this Issue" in *The Link (Americans for Middle East Understanding)* Vol. 25, No. 4 October/November 1992, p. 2. It is interesting to note that William Blackstone, the originator of the Blackstone Memorial that was detailed above, sent Louis Brandeis a packet of information on the forthcoming rapture, so he would be prepared. Accordingly, Blackstone claimed that Brandeis placed the information in his bank vault. This was following the Balfour Declaration and General Allenby's conquest of Jerusalem, which, according to Blackstone, was proof that the rapture was imminent. See *Prolegomena to Christian Zionism in America: The Views of Increase Mather and William E. Blackstone Concerning the Doctrine of the Restoration of Israel* (Ph.D. Diss., New York University, 1977), pp. 298-304. "Mather," in the titled of the noted book, was an early 18th Century American Puritan who wrote about the restoration of Israel in its ancient homeland. See ibid. Cf. 60. In regards to Brandeis, it is also claimed that "large sums of money" was sent to him from Blackstone during their twenty plus years of working together on behalf of Zionism. See, for instance, in P. C. Merkley, *The Politics of Christian Zionism 1891-1948* (London: Frank Cass, 1998), p. 14.

22 The Crusaders, who were Christian, captured Jerusalem in the First Crusade that began in 1099 by Godfrey of Bouillon. For nearly 200 years the Christians controlled the land until conquered in 1187 by Salah al-Din (Saladin), a Muslim. Jerusalem virtually stayed in the hands of Muslims (including during the Mameluke reign who converted to Islam), until 1917 when the British conquered the land. See Nitza Rosovsky; *City of the Great King: Jerusalem from David to the Present* (Harvard University Press: Cambridge, 1996), pg. 5-24

23 Congressional Record House "National Home for the Jewish People" House Resolution 360 (Rept. NO. 1172), p. 9811.

24 It is interesting to note that the Balfour Declaration was pronounced during General Allenby's march into Holy Land. Chaim Weizmann, in his trial and errors, poignantly points this out. See Weizmann, *Trial and Error* (New York: Harper, 1949), p. 200.

25 *Simon Glazer Papers*, Box titled "Lodge-Fish Resolution," American Jewish Archives, Cincinnati, OH, 1923, p. 102.

26 In 1915, Wilson's Secretary of State, William Bryan, directed Henry Morgenthau, who was the ambassador of Turkey, to convey the American sentiments to the proper Turkish authorities. See Jacob de Haas, *Louis D. Brandeis: A Biographical Sketch* (New York, 1929, p. 81. See also Charles Israel Goldblatt, "The Impact of the Balfour Declaration in America," in *American Jewish Historical Quarterly* (1967-1968) #57, pp. 457-458. Some of the forthcoming newspaper citations were taken from this essay.

27 It is well known that Brandeis played a significant role in many US government officials endorsement of Zionism, both in and out of the White House. See Louis Lipsky, *Thirty Years of American Zionism* vol. I (New York, 1927), pp. 65-72. More will be said later of Brandeis.

28 *New York Herald*, April 14, 1917.

29 From the New York *Evening Globe*, Nov. 12, 1917, cited in Goldblatt, "The Impact of the Balfour Declaration in America," p. 460.

30 *Dayton News*, May 14, 1918, *Kansas City Times*, May 18, 1918.

31 *The Boston Transcript*, Dec. 12, 1917, asserts this.

32 *Guardian* (Patterson, N.J.), Dec. 19, 1917.

33 *Courier* (Waterloo, Iowa), Dec. 11, 1917.

34 *Continent*, (New York City), Dec. 27, 1917.

35 *Times* (Denver, CO), May 8, 1918.

36 Such as the *Times* of St. Louis, Missouri, Dec. 6, 1917.

37 *Appeal*, Memphis, Tenn., Dec. 1, 1918. The New York *Evening Post* uses the Rothschilds of France and Louis Brandeis of America as proof that one's patriotism should not be labeled dishonorable. See *Evening Post* (New York) Dec. 11, 1917. See also Charles Israel Goldblatt, "The Impact of the Balfour Declaration in America," Cf. p. 460.

38 Ibid., Charles Israel Goldblatt, "The Impact of the Balfour Declaration in America," p. 464.

39 *Survey*, vol. XLI (Dec. 28, 1918), pp. 391-393. This was followed by a statement in the *North American Review*, under the title "The Second Coming of Israel" and believed that only with a Jewish state can anti-Semitism be countered. *North American Review*, vol. CCXVII (Jan. 1923), pp. 84-95.

40 Morris R. Cohen, "Zionism: Tribalism or Liberalism?" in the *New Republic*, vol. XIV (March 2, 1918), pp. 141-42.

41 Albert T. Clay, Political Zionism," in *Atlantic Monthly*, vol. CXXVII (Feb., 1921), pp. 268-69.

42 *The New York Times*, Jan. 6, 1920.

43 The idea here being that the Jews, as a people, scattered throughout the world, is still very difficult to convert. Once they are in the same vicinity, however, it was believed that it would be easier to compel them to Christianity. See the Presbyterian periodical, *Assembly Herald*, vol. 24 (Feb. 1918), p. 106; *Lutheran Companion*, vol. 26 (March 16, 1918), p. 130.

44 *The Month*, vol. CXXXVI (Sep. 1920), pp. 168-69, 268.

45 *Continent*, vol. L (July 29, 1920), p. 975. It should be noted, and as Brandeis points out, the Reform movement asserted that Judaism was a religion, not a nationality. Therefore, Reform stated that Jews were not "hyphenated Americans" but, "Americans of the Jewish faith". See Philippa Strum, *Louis D. Brandeis: Justice for the People* (Cambridge, Mass.: Harvard University Press, 1984), p. 266; Arthur Hertzberg, *The Jews in America: Four Centuries of an Uneasy Encounter: A History* (New York: Simon & Schuster, 1989), pp. 222-25.

46 *Christian Century*, vol. 39 (July 13, 1922), pp. 873-875.

47 *The New York Times*, Nov. 6 1922. Note that this article was a little more than a month after the passing of the Palestine Lodge-Fish Resolution.

48 *American Hebrew* (Nov. 16, 1917). King Cyrus of Persia issued an edict (circa 538 BCE) permitting Jews to return to the land of Israel and rebuild the Temple. The Temple, in Jerusalem, was destroyed (circa 586 BCE) by the Babylonians.

49 *Jewish Exponent* (Nov. 16, 1917).

50 A. Link, ed., *The Papers of Woodrow Wilson, vol. 49*, pp. 363-364. Several months later, in March 1919, Wilson noted that the letter had his "personal approval of the declaration of the British Government regarding Palestine." Jacob De Haas, *Louis D. Brandeis*, (Slusser Press, 2007) p.109.

51 Congressional Record House "National Home for the Jewish People" House Resolution 360 (Rept. NO. 1172), p. 9805.

52 It will be shown later that Brandeis had a large role to play in easing off Reform anti-Zionism, especially in the 1930s. Internal Reform politics changed, as did facts on the ground, notably Hitler's rise to power and the looming Jewish refugee problems

of the later 1930s, which was only exacerbated when World War II commenced. More will be said later about the Reform turnaround in regards to Zionism.

53 Charles Israel Goldblatt, "The Impact of the Balfour Declaration in America," p. 477.

54 *Dos Diddishes Tageblatt*, Nov. 8 and 18, 1917, Sept. 5, 1918.

55 *Der Forvertz* (Forward), Nov. 24, 1917.

56 See, for instance, C. Bezalel Sherman, Nationalism, Secularism, and Religion in the Jewish Labor Movement," in *Judaism*, vol. 3 (Fall, 1954), p. 355.

57 One group refused to accept that the redemption would transpire though a secular political movement, while others rejected Zionism on theological grounds, namely the Three Oaths, even though both concepts can be supported theologically or through the eyes of Judaism. Many believed the Oaths were not binding, or that they were allegorical, or that they had been abrogated by the Gentile nations themselves for not honoring their part of the agreement, namely not to "excessively" persecute the Jews (this is all pre-WWII, Holocaust discussion. After the Holocaust conversations about excessive force by the Gentiles only reinforced this idea). Hence, for many who asserted that the Oaths were binding, and who asserted that the Gentiles broke the agreement with their persecution, the Jews' were no longer bound to honor their Oaths since the contract had become null and void. See Paul Azous, *In the Plains of the Wilderness: Anthologies of Modern Jewish History* (Mazo Publishers, Jerusalem: 2006), pp. 123-128.

58 However, some mainstream Orthodox groups, such as the Agudath Yisrael, opposed Zionism so vehemently that some of their leaders claimed that Zionism is "The most formidable enemy that has ever arisen among the Jewish people."

59 Originally stated in 1913, this idea would be reiterated numerous times. From the Central Conference of American Rabbis Year Book, vol. 27 (Philadelphia: Jewish Publication Society of America), p. 132. Henry Morgenthau, as noted earlier, was a main leader of Reform opposition to Zionism. Following the successful lobbying of the US Congress, and even after the passing of the Balfour Declaration, Morgenthau's sentiments summed up his movement's feelings: "The Jews of France have found France to be their Zion. The Jews of England have found England to be their Zion. We Jews of America have found American to be our Zion. Therefore, I refuse to allow myself

to be called a Zionist. I am an American." Quoted in Henry Morgenthau, *All in a Lifetime* (Garden City, NY: 1922), p. 104. More on Morgenthau will be said in the chapters dealing with Jewish and Reform opposition to Zionism following the passing of the Palestine Resolutions of 1922.

60 Some of the aforementioned information, including this idea, is pointed out by Goldblatt, "The Impact of the Balfour Declaration in America," p. 483.

61 *The New York Times*, March 5, 1919.

62 Stephen S. Wise, "The Balfour Declaration: Its Significance in the USA," in *The National Home*, ed. Paul Goodman (London, 1943), p. 42. Cited in Goldblatt, "The Impact of the Balfour Declaration in America," p. 487.

63 The next several paragraphs, with variations, was taken from ibid.

64 Cited in *The New York Times*, March 3, 1919.

65 David Hunter Miller, *My Diary at the Conference of Paris: Policy towards Palestine*, vol. 4 (New York, 1924), pp. 263-64. Cited in Goldblatt, "The Impact of the Balfour Declaration in America," p. 493.

66 Ibid., from a letter the Zionist Organization of America sent to member of Congress. The noted numbers were the ones that replied. It is also noted in the work that the division between Republican and Democrat is virtually absent on the Zionist issue, where it appears that both sides equally supported the Balfour Declaration, and that, as some have erroneously maintained, there was no need for these members, at this time at least, to solicit Jewish votes for forthcoming elections. Although this view was maintained by the American Israelite newspaper that wrote "That we suspect that this will be used as a quiet intimation to each Congressman that unless he replies and his answer is such as is approved by their leaders, the Zionists of the country will work for his defeat at the polls next November." See *American Israelite*, Aug. 1, 1919.

67 From the British Foreign Office, November 2nd, 1917, the Balfour Declaration reads: "Dear Lord Rothschild: I have much pleasure in conveying to you. on behalf of His Majesty's Government, the following declaration of sympathy with Jewish Zionist aspirations which has been submitted to, and approved by, the Cabinet: His Majesty's Government view with favor the establishment in Palestine of a national home for the Jewish people, and will use their best endeavors to facilitate

the achievement of this object, it being clearly understood that nothing shall be done which may prejudice the civil and religious rights of existing non-Jewish communities in Palestine, or the rights and political status enjoyed by Jews in any other country. I should be grateful if you would bring this declaration to the knowledge of the Zionist Federation. Yours, Arthur James Balfour." For more on the Balfour Declaration, see Leonard Stein, *The Balfour Declaration* (London, Vallentine, Mitchell, 1961).

68 The Sykes-Picot was drafted in 1915 and approved in January 1916 by Russia, yet was not ratified until May of the same year. Under the Sykes-Picot agreement, the territory of Palestine mostly fell under British control except for a small section of the country north of a line from Acre to the north end of Lake Galilee (Tiberius). Religious sites, such as the Holy Sepulcher in Jerusalem, also fell under the sole jurisdiction of England. However, Jerusalem as a whole would fall under the jurisdiction of the British, French, and Russians. For more on this, see Walter Laqueur, *A History of Zionism*, p. 190.

69 Although the Ottomans conquered Palestine in 1517, it was not until 1841 that the Turks were granted complete control over the land. There were also instances where the Turks both lost and gained territory. For more on the historical background of the Ottoman conquest of Palestine, as well as the early Jewish communities under their control, see Jacob Barnai, *The Jews in Palestine in the Eighteenth Century Under the Patronage of the Istanbul Committee of Officials for Palestine*, trans. by Naomi Goldblum, pp. 11-24. For a thorough history of the struggle for control of the Middle East, see Isaiah Friedman, "Efraim and Inari Karsh, Empires of the Sand: The Struggle for Mastery in the Middle East, 1789-1923" in *Israel Studies* Volume 7, Number 1 (Spring 2002), pp. 222-230.

70 See Neville Mandel's, "Turks, Arabs and Jewish Immigration into Palestine, 1882-1914," in *"St. Anthony's Papers*, no. 17, *Middle Eastern Affairs* (Oxford: 1965), pp. 77-108.

71 On this see "Nahman Syrkin, "The Jewish Problem and the Socialist Jewish State," in Marie Syrkin, Nahman Syrkin, *Socialist Zionist: A Biographical Memoir and Selected Essays* (New York: Herzl Press and Sharon Books, 1961), pp. 288-89; Arthur Herztberg, *The Zionist Idea*, pp. 331-350.

72 For a greater elaboration on Turkey in regards to the growth of Zionism, see Isiah Friedman, *Germany, Turkey, and Zionism, 1897-1918* (Oxford, Clarendon, 1977).

73 For a comprehensive work on Arab nationalism, see Bernard Lewis, *The Shaping of the Modern Middle East* (New York and Oxford: Oxford University Press, 1994), pp. 71-163.

74 The estimated population of Palestine in 1922 was as follows: Jews constituted 83,000 souls, Muslims constituted 589,000 and Christians 71,000. See Paul Mendes Flohr and Jehuda Reinharz, *The Jew in the Modern World*, p. 705.

75 In an exchange of letter between 1915 and 1916, McMahon guaranteed Ali of Mecca that those Arab "countries" that aided the Allies in the war, especially against Turkey, would be granted independence. Many in the Arab world used the McMahon-Hussein correspondence to disclaim the implications of the Balfour Declaration. For more, see Paul Mendes Flohr and Jehuda Reinharz, *The Jew in the Modern World*, p. 592 note 1 and 4. England had numerous reasons for promising Ali a grand Arab state, most obviously an alliance with Mecca would ultimately weaken the Ottoman Empire, who controlled Arabia at the time. England was also cognizant of the vast oil reserves produced in Arabia, which could be used for war purposes at some future date. It should be noted that an area several kilometers north of Tel Aviv to the River Jordan and south along the Jordan Valley, which included the vicinity of Jerusalem, was to remain in British hands. Also, holy places would remain under English protection. For a map of Palestine, including how it affected the Mandate, see J. Stoyanovsky, *The Mandate for Palestine* (London, New York, Toronto, 1928), pp. 66, 204-210.

76 On the aforementioned treaties, see Rashid Khalidi, *British Policy towards Syria and Palestine 1906-1914: A Study of the Antecedents of the Hussein-McMahon Correspondence, the Sykes-Picot Agreement and the Balfour Declaration* (London, Ithaca Press, 1980).

77 For instance, "homeland" was interpreted as 1) a British protectorate 2) an autonomous Jewish region, yet "owned" by the British, and 3) a Jewish state. Chaim Weizmann, the head of the WZO, used the phrase "Jewish commonwealth" to describe the inference of the Balfour Declaration, setting off a storm among British politicians, as it jumped to final status negotiations. It should be noted that the first draft of the Declaration (July 1917), stated that "Her Majesty's Government accepts the principle *that* Palestine should be reconstituted..." the key word here being "that'. Several months later, in August, a similar version was drafted. However, the final version, released in November 1917, changed the wording to

the following: "His Majesty's Government view with favor the establishment *in* Palestine as a national home..." the key word here being "in". The difference of course is the eventual size of this Jewish national home. The final draft was drawn up with the help of Edwin Montagu, a Jew in the British Parliament who was a staunch opponent of Zionism. Apparently, he was fearful of being accused of having dual loyalties. The background of the Balfour Declaration, including opposition by Jews, played a significant role in the American version of 1922.

78 This later included League of Nations ratification. See League of Nations, Mandate for Palestine, Command #1785, Article 6, 1922.

79 For an elaboration, see Melvin Urofsky, *American Zionism from Herzl to the Holocaust* (Lincoln, Nebraska and London: University of Nebraska Press, 1995), p. 113.

80 Haycraft was then Chief Justice of Palestine and was appointed by High Commissioner Samuel. He found that Arab discontent, specifically in regards to Jewish immigration and Zionist policies, led to Arab rioting. The riots began in February 1920 in the Galilee, which eventually engulfed parts of Jerusalem, and the Tel Aviv area, i.e. Petach Tikvah, Hadera, Rehovot and other small settlements.

81 The Churchill White Paper had several significant points: 1) Britain reconfirms the Balfour Declaration, yet stipulates that they never did "contemplate that Palestine as a whole should be converted into a Jewish national home, but that such a home should be founded in Palestine"; 2)Trans-Jordan, i.e., the east bank, would not be open to Jewish immigration; 3) The number of Jewish émigrés will be determined by the "economic absorptive capacity" of Palestine; 4) The creation of separate Jewish and Arab governing councils to manage their own affairs would be set and; 5) A legislative Council consisting of Jews, Muslims and Christians as well a British delegates would be set up. For more on this see Anglo-American Committee, Survey, 1945-1956, vol. I, p. 20. It should be added that this White Paper basically created the future Kingdom of Jordan.

82 The Weizmann-Brandeis dispute is known as "the Split" and is mentioned only in the editorials of *The Herzlite*, a 1920s journal.

83 Chaim Weizmann, *Trial and Error: The Autobiography of Chaim Weizmann* (Philadelphia: The Jewish Publication Society of America, 1949), vol. 2, p. 267.

84 Brandeis believed that the American capitalist model was the

most suitable for the *Yishuv*, that simply donating money for causes, though part of American values as well, would only hamper the *Yishuv's* progress. The American Zionist position, as opposed to Eastern Europe, for instance, asserted that the Jews must create a democratic and capitalist society, as opposed to a socialist state that many Eastern European Jews, both in the Soviet Union and in the *Yishuv*, supported. See Yonathan Shapiro, *The Formative Years of the Israeli Labour Party: The Organization of Power 1919-1930* (London: Sage Publications, 1976), p. 73.

85 Brandeis, among other objections, also believed that Weizmann's proposed budget was inflated. See, for instance, Yonathan Shapiro, *Leadership*, pp. 161-79; Melvin I. Urofsky, *American Zionism from Herzl to the Holocaust* (Garden City, N.Y.: Anchor Press, 1975).

86 For more on the history of the Keren Hayasod debate, see *The Letters and Papers of Chaim Weizmann Vol. X, July 1920 - December 1921*, ed. Bernard Wasserstein (Transaction Books, Rutgers University, Israel University Press, Jerusalem, 1977), p. xii-xiii. Some of the forthcoming information is taken, with variation, from this work. It should be noted that the Keren Hayasod was the major supplier of funds to the Jewish Agency, after its creation in 1929. Aside from the United States where the United Jewish Appeal became the largest source of monetary aid to the *Yishuv*, Keren Hayasod was, in every other country, the dominant organization for collecting Zionist funds.

87 In a letter found in the Weizmann Archives, Weizmann writes that at a private lunch in hosted by Balfour's home, Lloyd George and Churchill both agreed that Balfour Declaration called for an eventual Jewish state. Ibid. p. 19.

88 In the June 1920 draft, Article 3 states that the Mandatory authorities will "secure the establishment of the Jewish National Home and the development of a self-governing commonwealth…" In the second draft of October 1920, it is stated that the Mandatory authorities "will secure the establishment of the Jewish National Home as laid down in the preamble, and the development of self governing institutions…" key difference being "self governing commonwealth" in the first draft compared with "self governing institutions" in the second. In the third and final draft of June 1922, the Mandatory authorities were supposed to "secure the establishment of the Jewish national home, as laid down in the preamble and the development of self governing

institutions..." Note that "Jewish national home", as opposed to the first two drafts, are not capitalized in the draft. The preambles to the clause Articles of all three drafts were also somewhat significantly changed. On July 24, 1922 the League of Nations, for the most part, followed the text of the draft sent by the British in December 1920. For the political and practical consequences of the various drafts, see Ben Halpern, *The Idea of the Jewish State* (London, 1970).

89 Wasserstein, *The Letters of Chaim Weizmann*, no. 7, 8 August, 1920, pp. xiv-xv.

90 Norman Rose, *Chaim Weizmann: A Biography* (New York: Viking Press, 1986), p. 210.

91 Ibid. letters no. 154, 180. In the latter letter, Weizmann writes that 95% of American Jews are ready to give to the Zionism that he is purporting, and that the vast majority of American Jews do not support the Brandeis approach to the movement.

92 The vote was 153 to 71 in support of Weizmann's initiative. See ibid. p. xvii.

93 Weizmann wrote on June 24, 1921, that "a rupture between the WZO and the American leaders was inevitable, nay, almost necessary, in order to bring about the establishment of the Fund in America and the creation of a real Zionist movement." Ibid., letter 204, p. xvii.

94 For more on Judge Mack and his Zionism, see Harry Barnard, *The Forging of an American Jew: The Life and Times of Judge Julian Mack* (New York: Herzl Press, 1974), pp. 36-44.

95 Louis Lipsky Papers, Box 1920-1922, American Jewish Historical Society, P- 672.

96 Today, the World Zionist Organization (WZO) maintains that the resignations, or even the ousting, of the most prominent American Zionists from the movement weakened development in the *Yishuv* in the 1920s, to the extent that the infrastructure, without American oversight, stagnated. Their website states the following: "It was years before American Zionism recovered (that is, with the absence of the "best minds of Zionism") from this setback; in fact not before Stephen Wise, Judge Mack and a few others had returned to active Zionist work." See http:// www.wzo.org.il/en/resources/view.asp?id=1635. The WZO is partially correct in their assumption. In 1929, the Zionist Organization of America had less than 18,000 members. With the rise of Hitler and the eventual news of the Final Solution, American Jewry would again become a compelling force in Zionist politics.

97 George L. Berlin, "The Brandeis-Weizmann Dispute," in *American Jewish Historical Quarterly* 60 (1970-1971): p. 37, 40.

98 Philippa Strum, *Louis D. Brandeis: Justice for the People* (Cambridge, Mass.: Harvard University Press, 1984), p. 256. Felix Frankfurter, at the Cleveland Conference, notes that he had to defend Brandeis from those wishing to attack his "Jewishness", as many claimed that a central component was absent from Brandeis's attitude, namely *Yiddishkeit*. Frankfurter responded that Moses was raised as an Egyptian prince, with idolatry constantly surrounding him. However, Moses still discovered his people and religion. Frankfurter remarked: "But so did Moses, raised as an Egyptian Prince." See Harry Barnard, *The Forging of an American Jew: The Life and Times of Judge Julian W. Mack* (New York: Herzl Press, 1974), p. 281.

99 Zionist Organization of America, *Brandeis on Zionism: A Collection of Addresses and Statements by Louis D. Brandeis* (New York: H. Wolff, 1942), p. 29.

100 This idea was expressed by Menahem Ussishkin. See Urofsky, *American Zionism*, Cf. 295; see also Urofsky's analysis of American and European culture on pp. 283-98.

101 Glazer wrote that the reason for Weizmann's attendance was because "The situation being so critical, every possible help was needed." See *Simon Glazer Papers*, American Jewish Archives, Box entitled "Lodge of Palestine Resolution" pp. 2-3.

102 Ibid. p. 4.

103 Ibid.

104 It should be noted that the United States recommended at the Paris Peace Conference, January 21, 1919 "That there be established a separate state of Palestine.... placed under Great Britain as a mandatory of the League of Nations ... that the Jews be invited to return to Palestine and settle there.... and being further assured that it will be the policy of the League of Nations *to recognize Palestine as a Jewish state as soon as it is a Jewish state in fact.* . . . England, as mandatory, can be relied on to give the Jews the privileged position they should have without sacrificing the [religious and property] rights of non-Jews." Although not official American policy, as that wouldn't transpire for several years, it was regarded by the Zionist movement as significant. See also US Congressional Resolution, June 30, 1922, in Survey of Palestine, p. 1.

105 Established under the tutelage of Tsar Nicholas I (1825-1855), the cantonist system (meaning "juvenile conscripts") was

developed to break the Jewish connection to Judaism and supplant it with Russian mores. Military service, coupled with the ideals of Russian education and culture, devastated many Jewish communities. Consequently, Jews were forbidden to speak Yiddish while in the cantonists. They were also forced to have lessons in Christianity. To exacerbate the situation, the Russian authorities forced the rabbinic leaders to hand pick many of the Jewish recruits. The "Khapers" as they were called, often apprehended from their families boys as young as eight years old and place them in the proper Russian authorities. The Russians succeeded in weakening the Jewish political establishment as well as break many Jews' connection to Judaism. An estimated 40-50,000 Jewish youth were taken before the law was revoked in 1859. For more, see Paul Mendes Flohr and Jehuda Reinharz, *The Jew in the Modern World* (Oxford and New York, Oxford University Press, 1980), pp. 377-87, esp. note 1.

106 However, a short archival biography of Glazer, this one found in Seattle, Washington, claims that he arrived in America 1896. See "Simon Glazer," in *The Jewish Voice of the Pacific Coast*, April 26, 1918 and August 14, 1918, p. 1. Many thanks to Meta R. Buttnick of Seattle who graciously sent me archival information from Congregation Bikkur-Cholim-Machzikay Hadath of Seattle, including the aforementioned information. It should be noted that Glazer's archival works can be broken down into three sections with corresponding time frames. First is Glazer's writing on the Sioux City, Iowa Jews from 1869-1904; he wrote a history of this small, but significant Jewish community. Secondly, and most significantly, are Glazer's writings, his lectures, letters he wrote and received, and selections of his diary where he expressed a deep desire to help the Jewish nation acquire its homeland. Most of this box can be broken down into several folders, including "The Lodge Palestine Resolution," "The Beth El Jewish Collection Lectures," which are a collection of his speeches, both politically and religiously oriented. "The Zionist Organization of America," "The Charles Curtis Papers, 1921-1932," and the "Proposed Constitution for Palestine," are letters of correspondence between Glazer and many prominent figures in the political arena. To Glazer, himself a "pioneer" to Palestine in 1897, the Halutzim had "spirit and wisdom" and they were "worthy of the descendants of the Maccabeans."

107 When Glazer came to Palestine in 1897, fewer than 100,000

Jews were settled throughout the country. Those who stayed and continued to build the desolate land left a lasting, positive impression on Glazer. This influence can be seen from a letter of correspondence that Glazer received from the Zionist Organization of America on November 9, 1921, where the sender, Louis Lipsky, the Secretary of the ZOA, implies that he sympathizes with Glazer about the pioneers who "still give their life for the land." See SGP Box 269 Section 2/3 "The Proposed Constitution for Palestine," p. 6. He therefore felt compelled to help his brethren attain the Holy Land, and in so doing, he continued, the Jews would achieve salvation from Heaven. On this, see again "Simon Glazer," in *The Jewish Voice of the Pacific Coast*, Newspaper, April 26, 1918 and August 14, 1918, p. 1.

108 SGP Box 269 Section 2/1, Folder entitled "Glazer's Discourses on Civil Law," American Jewish Archives (AJA), Introduction.

109 Glazer, Simon, *The Jews of Iowa*. Koch Bros. Printing Co. (Des Moines: 1904), Chapter 21, p. 5.

110 Ibid.

111 Ibid. He later writes that even though the Reform Jews have done away with most of the central and ancient Jewish traditions, they are the most proud of their ancestry in the state of Iowa. See also Bernard Shuman, *A History of the Sioux Jewish Community: 1869-1969* (Iowa: Jewish Federation of Sioux City, 1969), Introduction.

112 While serving the Seattle Jewish community, Glazer is said to have spoken English so well that a trace of European accent could not be found. See the "Anches Interview," Washington State Jewish Historical Society (WSJHS) Archive, University of Washington, November 24, 1981.

113 Moshe D. Sherman, *Orthodox Judaism in America: A Biographical Dictionary and Sourcebook* (Connecticut and London: Greenwood Press, 1996), p. 76.

114 See Meta Buttnick, "Congregation Bikkur-Cholim-Machzikay Hadath of Seattle: The Beginning years," *Western States Jewish History, Vol. 22*, Section dealing with the years 1915-1925.

115 "The Consensus of Civil Judaism: The Religious Life of Kansas City Jewry," in Joseph P. Schult, ed., *Mid-America's Promise: A Profile of Kansas City Jewry* (Kansas City, 1982). Although Glazer is mentioned only one time in this work, the author praises him for his civil discourses. It is noteworthy to add that, while in Kansas City, Glazer was also instrumental in creating the

United Synagogue, a system of Jewish centralization regarding communal affairs. For instance, the United Synagogue inspected kosher food and placed price limits on Passover goods. See Sherman, *Orthodox Judaism in America*, p. 76.

116 Such as, for instance, when Glazer wrote a scathing letter to a Joe Teich of Kansas City who refused to send for his wife and children in Europe while he remarried in America. In a stern tone, Glazer demanded to see him at once. See SGP Box 269 1/17 entitled "The Zionist Organization of America," letter dated September 6, 1922 from Glazer to Teich.

117 The ZOA also asked Glazer for help in a number of serious problems that arose. One crisis that occurred was in 1922, prior to the US declaration supporting Zionism. The ZOA attempted to combat anti-Zionist propaganda that was being distributed by Europeans anti-Semites and Arab Muslims who campaigned for the rescinding of the Balfour Declaration. In a number of letters, Glazer was implored to help. The tone of the letters reflects an atmosphere of fright, entreating him for assistance. Glazer also rallied support from international Jewish communities. One example was his effort to assemble international support for the implementation of the Balfour Declaration from groups in Canada. "Mercaz HaRabbanim D'America VeKanada" Simon Glazer Papers (SGP) Box 269 1/5 Section Entitled "Charles Curtis – 1921-1932," dated Feb. 8, 1928.

118 The name "Mizrahi" has its roots from the Hebrew words *merkaz ruhani*, "spiritual center." It was created by Rabbi Meir Berlin (Bar Ilan), who used it to express the movements meaning: "The Land of Israel for the people of Israel according to the Torah of Israel." Mizrahi was founded in 1902 as a religious faction in the World Zionist Organization. Shmuel Mohilever, an early leader of Hibbat Zion, to express the idea that Torah should be the spiritual center for Zionism, first used the name. See *Encyclopedia Judaica* (Jerusalem: Keter Publishing House Jerusalem Ltd., 1972), Section entitle "Mizrahi."

119 See again the "Anches Interview," Washington State Jewish Historical Society (WSJHS) Archive, University of Washington, November 24, 1981. Glazer was known as a "student of the Rambam (Maimonides)". He was one of the first to translate Maimonides' entire *Mishnah Torah* into English.

120 Glazer was a trusted confidant of Mizrahi, at least by 1918. I was unable to find out exactly when or under what circumstances he became acquainted with the organization. In

a letter addressed to the President of the United States, Mizrahi implores him to intervene "on behalf of our unfortunate brethren" who were being "massacred plundered, raped, and hounded by a systematic campaign of boycott and persecution" that "has ensued against the Jews." Glazer and four other representatives singed off on the letter. See SGP Box 269 Section 1/17, 1921-1923, p. 90 (last page of section). This note is written for two reasons: First, to show that Glazer was actually a trusted confidant of Mizrahi. Second, to show that Glazer fought for all types of Jewish rights, not just for religious and communal liberties but for the actual, physical safety of Jews anywhere. Although Mizrahi was an Orthodox Zionist organization, they never refrained from helping Jews that were not part of the Zionist movement as well as those who did not intend to move to the Land of Israel. Although this is referenced in one of Glazer's letters that he received, there are no names listed. The letter was dated November 10, 1923, which by this time, Glazer was very familiar with most leading Orthodox Zionist leaders. See SGP Box 269, Section 2/1, Entitled "Hebrew Manuscripts."

121 SGP Box 269 Section 2/3, Entitled "The Lodge of Palestine Resolution" p. 11. This section deals with the "Palestine Resolution" and is most fascinating, and many more citations will come from it. This section is also found in the "Beth El Jewish Collection Lectures, 1928," although this can be a bit misleading. Most of Glazer's lectures were given or written prior to 1928, but in this year they were compiled.

122 GP Box 2692/3 entitled "The Proposed Constitution for Palestine," 1920-1921, p. 11.

123 This group, of course, uses the Babylonian Talmud, Tractate *Ketuvoth* 111a as their source for not returning to the land of Israel prior to the Messiah's arrival. Here the Talmud discusses the *Shelosh Shavuot*, the Three Oaths, one of them being "not to hasten the End," a reference interrupted by the opponents of Zionism referring to hastening of the Messianic Era by returning to the land of Israel.

124 SGP Box 269 Section 2/3, Entitled "The Lodge of Palestine Resolution" p. 3.

125 Glazer points out that had the World Zionist Organization, headed by Chaim Weizmann, failed to bring the Balfour Declaration into being, then Great Britain would have invited the Agudath Yisrael into the "Jewish Cabinet" that would then decide the fate of the Balfour Declaration. Glazer reasons

that this is similar to other localities around the world where the British control. Had one "cabinet" failed to do its job, the British would invite in the opposition. This, Glazer wrote, would have been a disaster "because the Agudath are opposed to Zionism." See SGP Box 2692/3 entitled "The Proposed Constitution for Palestine," 1920-1921, p. 20. On the Agudath Yisrael, See Sherman, *Orthodox Judaism in America*, pp. 245-246.

126 Ibid. Here Glazer says that "The Balfour Declaration carried terror in their midst, as they interpreted it to give dual citizenship to the Jewish people the world over." It should be noted that during this time period, roughly from 1920-1922, Glazer was strenuously lobbying all parts of the American government to create a resolution similar to the position that Great Britain took regarding the Jewish claim to Palestine in the Balfour Declaration.

127 "Simon Glazer," in *The Jewish Voice of the Pacific Coast*, Newspaper, April 26, 1918 and August 14, 1918, p. 1. Anyone who has spent time learning with a Rosh Yeshiva (the head of a Jewish academy of higher learning), or one who considers a certain rabbi his "Master" can attest that a person's Rebbe molds one's outlook in regards to Torah and in many respects, his worldview, regardless of the generation or era. This certainly holds true for Glazer and Rabbi Lapidot. Rabbit Lapidot wrote that "All that we want is solely to create a group of farmers who will work the earth, firmly settled in Eretz Israel, to which we are connected by thousands of years of history and which was destined to us by G-d through the intermediary of the holy prophets. It is a very great mitzvah to settle there." For more on Rabbi Lapidot, see D. Katz, *Tenu'at ha-Musar*, 2 (1964), 436–8; M. Markovitch, *Le-Korot Ir Rosyan ve-Rabbaneha* (1913), 14–16.

128 Although *Mikve Israel* was the first agricultural settlement created in Palestine 1870 in Petach Tikveh (with the help of the *Alliance Israelite Universalle*, and a leading religious Zionist thinker Rabbi Tzvi Kalischer) it was still not a school that could produce the necessary tools to expand the *Yishuv's* objectives. This can be seen from the Palestine Jewish Colonization Society in a letter of complaint to their financial backers in Europe. See Simon Schama, *Two Rothchilds and the Land of Israel* (New York: Alfred A. Knopf, 1978), p. 168.

129 For Hadassah, this one was of the great milestones for their policy of Practical Zionism.

130 Hadassah Magazine, March 2002, Vol. 83 No. 7 p. 2. As the
leading Zionist women's organization (back in the early days
of the *Yishuv* as well as today) Hadassah claims that their aim
is still Practical Zionism, and has little to do with the political
aspects of the State of Israel. "Practical Zionism emphasized
practical means of attaining Zionist goals, such as *aliyah*
(immigration), rural settlement and educational institutions,
despite inadequate political conditions. This approach
originated in the *Hibbat Zion* movement in the 1880s, well before
Political Zionism. After Theodor Herzl's death in 1904, as hopes
of obtaining a charter in Palestine were dashed, and after the
Uganda Proposal controversy of 1903, Practical Zionism, calling
for the intensification of rural settlement in Palestine, gained
strength. The champions of this doctrine were the members of
the Second *Aliyah* who settled in Palestine at this time. They
founded rural settlements, some along cooperative principles;
built modern towns; and established the first industrial
enterprises. The 1907 decision to establish the Palestine office of
the Zionist movement in Jaffa, headed by Dr. Arthur Ruppin,
further reinforced this approach." See http://www.us-israel.
org/jsource/Zionism.html. This can be seen from as early
as 1917 where Glazer met with numerous public officials in
Missouri. He subsequently met with the same officials and
their successors. See the "Lodge of Palestine Resolution" p. 5.
Also, Glazer points that even by November 13, 1908, Senator
Albert Cummins had met with him and pledged his support
in giving "all the influence I have toward the enactment of
such laws as you suggest, and more than that, to any other
law that will ensure impartial civic treatment in every part
of the world towards the Jewish race." I am convinced that
when Cummins refers to "every part of the world," he is
referring to the treatment of Palestinian Jews, who were being
mistreated by the Ottomans, and strangely, the Syrians. In this
discourse, Glazer starts off his writings by saying that this "is a
complete report of my activities in connection with the political
situation of Palestine." See SGP Box 269 2/3 folder entitled
"Administrative Committee, Zionist Organization of America"
p. 2.

131 For more on the Ottoman (and later British) attitude towards
Jewish immigration see Nahman Syrkin, "The Jewish Problem
and the Socialist Jewish State," in Marie Syrkin, Nahman
Syrkin, *Socialist Zionist: A Biographical Memoir and Selected Essays*
(New York: Herzl Press and Sharon Books, 1961), pp. 288-89;

Arthur Herztberg, *The Zionist Idea* (Cleveland and New York The World Publishing Company and Jewish publication Society of America, 1959), pp. 331-350.

132 SGP Box 269 "The Proposed Constitution for Palestine" 2/3, p. 16. Here Glazer writes that "the greatest in connection with the establishment of a Jewish national home is the small Jewish population in Palestine." "The Proposed Constitution for Palestine" was either written in 1920 or 1921 and a copy of the printouts is found in Glazer's *History of Israel Vol.1*, (New York, 1930).

133 Ibid. p. 17.

134 Ibid. p. 17.

135 In Glazer's own words, the Jews found "themselves isolated socially and otherwise, although not openly attacked, they do not feel at home amidst such environment." The "environment" he is referring to is the European continent, and more specifically, England. See "The Proposed Constitution for Palestine" p. 6.

136 Ibid. p. 7.

137 He ends by saying that "This is the psychological reason why the Jewish masses are finding the British Empire a difficult if not impossible place." His special contempt for England can be shown all over his writings, and especially when he gives a history of "British Rule." In fact, Glazer believed that even during the most trying periods of European Jewish history, the Jews still did not move to England, rather they opted to move someplace more "appealing." See ibid. pp. 7-8.

138 Tsar Alexander III imposed the May Laws, on May 3, 1882. Prior to the enactment of these laws, pogroms broke out across Russia that devastated many Jewish communities and where civil unrest became all too common. An inquiry was sent to decipher why and under what circumstances the unrest began wherein the commission reported that the Jews were to blame. Alexander III, imposing decrees that his father Alexander II had retracted, such as the liberalizing of the Pale of Settlement, set out to punish the Jews for the unrest. Jews could not settle outside the Pale anymore (an act the Alexander II allowed in some cases), the registration of Jewish property and mortgages had to be halted, and they were no longer permitted, among others, to engage in business on Sundays and Christian holidays. For more, see Paul Mendes Flohr and Jehuda Reinharz, *The Jew in the Modern World*, p. 380.

139 Ibid. pp. 10-11. Glazer also said that France looks "indifferently" at the Jewish treatment by the hands of the Russians.

140 SGP Box 269 2/3 "The Lodge of Palestine Resolution" p. 11, also located in the "Beth El Jewish Collection Lecture", compiled 1928, folder entitled "Balfour Declaration." Although Glazer praises the British for their bold initiative, he also takes them to task for their "double treatment" of the Jews. See again "Balfour Declaration" folder.

141 Ibid. p. 11. Glazer further stated the belief that Great Britain was interested in a Jewish homeland, although at first it was not to be in Palestine but Uganda. The fact that the Uganda was even flirted with as a potential locality for a Jewish homeland, he reasoned, proved that England was serious about Jewish independence. It should be noted that although the country of Uganda is famously mentioned as the potential Jewish home in East Africa, in fact, it was present day Kenya that was proposed. The "East Africa" plan was commonly referred to by those in the Zionist movement as the "Uganda" proposal. The British, who offered part of East Africa to the Jews, did not specify the size or the exact location of the proposal. Joseph Chamberlain, future Prime Minister of England, spoke of the section of East Africa that would be allotted to the Jews that "lies between Nairobi and the Mau Escarpment," which is mostly in present day Kenya, not Uganda. For more on this, see R.G. Weisbord, *African Zion: The Attempt to Establish a Jewish Colony in the East African Protectorate 1903-1905* (Philadelphia: The Jewish Publication Society of America, 1968), pp. 1-33, 59-58. See also my "In the Plains of the Wilderness", pp. 114-115.

142 Ibid.

143 Ibid. p. 12.

144 Ibid.

145 Here Glazer also says that great sympathy for the Jewish people erupted in England following World War I, where the Jews "suffered great loses." See Ibid.

146 Ibid. p. 13. Glazer writes that no other Jewish leader had ever heard that Great Britain would make a pronouncement of this magnitude. He claims, as noted above, that Desola was the first one to hear that such a statement would be issued.

147 Ibid. p. 14.

148 Ibid.

149 SGP Box 269 2/3 "The Proposed Constitutions for Palestine" folder entitled "The Constitution," p. 1.

150 See the "Lodge of Palestine Resolution" p. 7. Throughout the "Lodge of Palestine Resolution" as well as many other documents, essays, and especially letters of correspondence, many US government officials speak in terms of Zionism as "a place where my Savior came from" or "the need for a Jewish homeland" as an alternative to living amongst the nations. The Bible is the most often used reason by non-Jewish authorities as to why the Jews should be granted Palestine.

151 This though, is not entirely accurate, as the emir of Arabia, Faisal, did negotiate with Weizmann. It was understood during the negotiations that the Zionist movement would obtain a significant amount of land in Palestine. See also my "In the Plains of the Wilderness", pp.120-122.

152 Here Glazer appears blunt when writing the Governor. The letter reads as though the Governor had no choice but to meet Glazer in the morning, and that the two were close. Indeed, many of his letters to Governor Allen reflect two old friends communicating with one another. See SGP Box 269 1/7 Folder entitled "The Zionist Organization of America," pp. 2-3.

153 Ibid. p. 3.

154 Glazer points out that Governor Allen was close friends with "one of the strongest men in America today," Charles Curtis, who was a close personal friend of President Harding and the Floor Leader of the United States Senate. Curtis, as will be shown, was instrumental in helping Glazer convince the President and Senate that a resolution like the Balfour Declaration be created and proclaimed in America. See ibid.

155 Ibid. p. 1.

156 SGP Box 269 1/17 entitled "The Zionist Organization of America," 1921-1923. Louis Lipsky, the General Secretary of the ZOA, sent this letter, dated March 3, 1922. The letter is thus far the strongest in terms of any organization or individual imploring Glazer for help.

157 Ibid.

158 Ibid.

159 Northcliffe was constantly known for ridiculing the ruling party in England. Even though he was disliked by many in the government, Prime Minister David Lloyd George, in December 1916, offered him a position in his cabinet. However,

Northcliffe refused. He felt that it would undermine his ability to criticize the government, like he did with the Balfour Declaration. Some of this information is scattered throughout the "Zionist Organization of America" as well as on the Web. See, for instance, http://www.spartacus.schoolnet.co.uk/BUharmsworth.htm.

160 SGP Box 269 1/17 entitled "Zionist Organization of America," Letter dated February 27, 1922 from Goldberg to Glazer.

161 It is not specified where the finances would be spent although I surmise that it would be used for colonization purposes.

162 Goldberg in his letter implies that those in the "Pro-Judaea" in Italy and Switzerland recited some type of prayer for the creation of a Jewish state. It may very well be that they recited portions of the Psalms. See again Goldberg's letter, dated February 27, 1922, found in the "Zionist Organization of America" 1/17.

163 This idea is found in several places noted early. See ibid. as well as the letter dated March 3, 1922, where both documents acknowledge that anti-Semitism and anti-Zionism must be fought.

164 SGP Box 269 1/17 "Zionist Organization of America" p. 55. This letter is dated July 11, 1921 and was sent once again by Louis Lipsky, the General Secretary of the ZOA, the same individual who earlier implored Glazer to garner support from the local and state newspapers in support of Zionism.

165 Ibid. Folder entitled "Administrative Committee, Zionist Organization of America," p. 5.

166 Ibid. p. 6.

167 Glazer also wrote that these "so-called Christian countries" were not true followers of Christianity, as true Christianity would not murder in the name of their God. See ibid.

168 Ibid.

169 Ibid. On September 29, 1921, approximately two weeks after McKelvie met with Glazer, he sent him a package. Enclosed in the package were copies of letters that McKelvie had sent to the two senators of Nebraska, Senator Hotchikess and Senator Norris, entreating both to support the Zionist movement.

170 SGP Box 269 1/17 entitled "Miscellaneous" where most of the fifty or so documents begin with "Western Union Telegram," Kansas City, Missouri, or New York, NY.

171 Ibid. Lipsky implies this in his telegram to Glazer.

Interestingly, Lipsky takes Glazer to task for allowing the ascension of Jacob Frankfurter to the Board of Electorates of Kansas City. Apparently, Frankfurter was opposed to Keren Hayesod and had a cool relationship with Zionism in general. Lipsky, upset by this happenstance, urges Glazer not to allow this to happen. Lipsky wrote that "if Zionists favor Keren Hayesod why allow or belove to appoint a delegate opposed to Keren Hayesod?"

172 Ibid., entitled "Keren Hayesod." In a letter dated October 5, 1921, Secretary of the Executive Committee, Bernard G. Richards commended Glazer for his role in raising needed funds for Keren Hayesod.

173 Ibid. Letter dated December 4, 1921. Although the actual dollar amount is not given, Nahum Sokolow, one of the leaders of the ZOA, recognized Glazer for his continued support for the cause.

174 In fact, it is quite possible that Glazer raised funds for Keren Hayesod right up until his death in 1938. Throughout the 1920s, Glazer was active all over New York on behalf of the Palestine Foundation Fund. For instance, on Shavuot of 1924, Glazer petitioned his congregation, Beth Hamedrash Hagodol of Harlem, insisting that his "flock" donate what they can to Keren Hayesod. Although no money changed hands on Shavuot do to the holiday strictures, Glazer was cautioned that the pledges made should be collected. See ibid., letter dated June 13, 1924 and signed off by Emanuel Neumann, Secretary of Keren Hayesod. Throughout the 1920's and 1930's, Glazer was recognized for many of his achievements, and was consistently recognized both by the ZOA and Keren Hayesod for his fundraising efforts. In many letters in the "Zionist Organization of America" section of the archives, as well as in several letters from Keren Hayesod, one finds documents conveying similar sentiments to Glazer "expressing dear appreciation of the splendid appeal(s)" that he made. See "Zionist Organization of America," letters dated December 4, 1921, December 22, 1921 (there are several letters to Glazer sent to him on this date), and March 23, 1923. As for "Keren Hayesod" see letters dated September 28, and December 1921, as well as June 13, 1921.

175 SGP Box 269 1/17, entitled "Zionist Organization of America," 1921-1923, pp. 10-13.

176 SGP Box 269 2/3, entitled "The Lodge of Palestine Resolution,"

pp. 1-2. Also found in the "Beth El Jewish Collection Lectures," 1928.

177 Ibid. p. 2.

178 Ibid.

179 The stigma that the Jews killed Jesus would never leave them. This stigma took on many forms. Theologically the Jews were branded as the devil in disguise. According to early Church Fathers, like St. Augustine, the Jews were branded with the mark of Cain, condemned forever to wander the earth; hence the land of Israel should never again come under Jewish control. See the writing of the 4th century St. Augustine in St. John Chrysostom in *Conflict of the Church and the Synagogue* (London, 1934), pp. 163-166.

180 "Lodge of Palestine Resolution," p. 2. Here Glazer writes that even the "harmless" elements in the Arab world had been penetrated by this Jew-hatred.

181 The "Czar like pogroms" Glazer refers to were the 1920 Arab riots against the Jews, first in the Galilee in March 1920, and then in the Old City of Jerusalem (known also as the Nebi Musa Riots). From April 4 to April 7, 1920 the Jewish Quarter of the Old City, including its shops and synagogues, were ransacked, while hundreds of Jews were physically assaulted, with five dead. It has been argued by numerous scholars, including Tom Segev, that General Allenby and his staff encouraged the attacks against the Jews, with the understanding that, for various reasons, "Jewish domination in Palestine" was undesirable. See, for instance, Richard Meinertzhagen, *Middle East Diary 1917-1956* (London, 1959), pp. 55-56.

182 "Lodge Palestine Resolution," p. 2.

183 Ibid.

184 Glazer attempts to prove his thesis by showing that the *chalutzim*, pioneers, both boys and girls, are still immigrating to Palestine, building roads and houses, planting trees and laying the foundation for "a university on Mt. Zion...which will perhaps be the greatest university of all ages." See Ibid.

185 Ibid. Glazer and other Zionist leaders were skeptical of the State Department's motives. Weizmann always had difficulty with the Department of State. See Chaim Weizmann, *Trial and Error* (New York: Harper, 1949), pp. 431-432.

186 Ibid. Glazer believed that the State Department was looking out for the interests of the United States. Glazer, of course believed

that Zionism's goal was in the best interest of the US.

187 Ibid. p. 5.

188 SGP Box 269 2/3 "The Lodge of Palestine Resolution," letter dated September 19, 1921 from Governor Allen to Glazer.

189 Ibid. Governor Allen mentioned that he will speak with Senator Arther Capper, who was one of the two senators from Kansas. Kapper had been a strong supporter of social reform throughout his career, and was a friend of the Jewish community of Kansas, which, incidentally, was strategic for Glazer's mission. See Homer E. *Arthur Capper, Publisher, Politician, and Philanthropist* (Lawrence: University of Kansas Press, 1962), Introduction.

190 "The Lodge of Palestine Resolution," letter dated September 13, 1921 from Senator Curtis to Governor Allen.

191 SGP Box 269 1/5 entitled "Charles Curtis," 1921-1932, letter dated September 12, 1921 from Senator Curtis to Governor Allen from the "United States Senate, Committee on Indian Affairs." The same letter is found in "The Lodge Palestine Resolution" with the same date. See note 101.

192 See "Administrative Committee, Zionist Organization of America, p. 4, letter dated September 19, 1921 from Senator Curtis to Governor Allen.

193 "The Lodge of Palestine Resolution" letter dated September 28, 1921 from Governor Hyde to Glazer.

194 Ibid. Note the two-fold reasons for Spencer's support of this resolution: 1) His Savior was Jew and 2) Jews deserve a home because of their suffering and persecution. These two reasons, as mentioned earlier, was the most consistent reasons given by Christians for supporting the creation of a Jewish homeland.

195 "The Palestine Lodge Resolution" p.4

196 Ibid. p. 7.

197 Ibid. Letter dated September 29, 1921 from Governor McKelvie to Glazer.

198 See "Administrative Committee, Zionist Organization of America," p. 7.

199 On September 23, Glazer received a letter from Curtis explaining the difficulty it is to meet with the Secretary of State. Time constraints and a host of other problems arose. He assured him though, that "as soon as I get a little time I will gladly call upon him and go over the situation with him fully,"

which he did. By the end of the month, Curtis had taken the resolution initiative as his own personal project. See "Charles Curtis" papers, letter dated September 23, 1921 entitled "United States Senate, Committee on Indian Affairs," from Curtis to Glazer.

200 "Administrative Committee, Zionist Organization of America" letter dated September 30, 1921 from Glazer to Harding. See also p. 7 where Glazer specifically makes reference to the Jewish suffering in the former war zones of Europe, which became independent nations where Jews still suffer.

201 Ibid.

202 "The Palestine Lodge Resolution," p. 7.

203 In fact, Secretary of State Robert Lansing advised President Wilson as early as 1917 that he should "go very slowly" in his encouragement of Zionism. See Frank E. Manuel, *The Realities of American-Palestine Relations* (Washington D.C.: Public Affairs Press, 1949), p. 172. Some, including Philip Baram, take Lansing to task for his "apologetic" stance of the State Department. He writes that even in Wilson's era and shortly after, the view in the State Department was that "the less the Department had to do with Zionist leaders the better." See Philip J. Baram, The *Department of State in the Middle East 1919-1945* (Philadelphia: University of Pennsylvania Press, 1978), p. 53. This same idea was reinforced by President Harding to Glazer in a letter dated October 13, 1921, where G. Christian, Jr. the Secretary to President Harding at the time, wrote that all "matters of ratifications of mandates and other affecting the former Ottoman empire, cannot for the moment be given definite action." Ironically, Glazer writes, "This pronouncement of the President was of the greatest benefit to the cause of Jewish freedom..." Apparently, Glazer believed that once a peace treaty was signed with Turkey, the United States would move on the Palestine issue. See ibid. p. 8.

204 See "Charles Curtis" papers, entitled "United States Senate, Committee on Indian Affairs," dated October 17, 1921 from Curtis to Glazer. Glazer was later informed that the President had made up his mind regarding Palestine that very same day.

205 "Administrative Committee, Zionist Organization of America" p. 8.

206 Ibid. p. 9.

207 Ibid. Letter dated October 21, 1921 from Allen to Glazer from the "Executive Department" of the State of Kansas.

208 Ibid. p. 10.

209 Ibid.

210 SGP Box 269 1/5 entitled "Charles Curtis" telegram dated November 12, 1921 from Curtis to Glazer.

211 Ibid. This telegram is also found in "Administrative Committee, Zionist Organization of America," p. 10.

212 "Charles Curtis," telegram dated November 14, 1921 from Curtis to Glazer. This telegram is also found in "Administrative Committee, Zionist Organization of America," p. 11.

213 "Administrative Committee, Zionist Organization of America," p. 11.

214 See "The Palestine Lodge Resolution," p. 9, letter dated November 17, 1921 from Senator Curtis to President Harding, "Administrative Committee, Zionist Organization of America," p. 12, and "Charles Curtis" papers, letter dated November 17, 1921 from Curtis to Harding, folder entitled "United States Senate, Committee on Rules." There is another letter written by Curtis to Harding dated also on November 17, yet worded differently. See again "Charles Curtis" papers.

215 "Administrative Committee, Zionist Organization of America," p. 12, in a conversation between Glazer and Harding. Harding replied, "It is very gracious of you to say so."

216 Ibid. p. 13.

217 Ibid.

218 Ibid.

219 President Harding said he would try and meet with Balfour at his earliest convenience with the intention of working with the British government on behalf of world Jewry. See ibid.

220 Ibid. p. 15. Glazer also told Harding another story, similar in tragedy, where a man, Helenko, in St. Louis, Missouri lost his wife and three children in Fastov.

221 Ibid.

222 Ibid. p. 16.

223 Ibid.

224 Ibid.

225 Ibid.

226 On November 19, 1921 *The New York Times* reported. The article heading was "Harding Lets Rabbi Adopt Five Orphans in Rumania". Here is the brief article:

WASHINGTON, Nov. 18, — President Harding gave Rabbi
Simon Glazer of Kansas City, Kan., *(sic)* executive permission
to adopt five children who are now in Rumania. The rabbi has
already five children, and the new additions are Jewish children
who were left orphans by the death of their mother in one of
the massacres in the Ukraine in 1920 and the death of their
father in the United States. Immigration restrictions would have
prevented them from coming to the United States, but President
Harding agreed to allow Rabbi Glazer to adopt them and thus
legalize their entry. The oldest is 17 and the youngest 9 years,
and a collection has been taken up in Kansas City to pay their
transportation expenses.

227 Ibid. It could very well be that when Harding told this to
Glazer, he may have been hinting that the Jews too will
remember him long after his political career ends.

228 "The Lodge of Palestine Resolution," p. 10. Letter dated
November 21, 1921 from Allen to Glazer.

229 "Administrative Committee, Zionist Organization of America,"
p. 17.

230 It is important to note that Glazer believed that the Arabs were
anti-Zionist and becoming virulently anti-Semitic because
of France, who in turn was backed by the Vatican. As long
as France, Glazer writes, "with all its frivolity, mirth in
worldliness, desires a share in Heaven in return for performing
a Catholic duty toward the backward races of the Near East
and as she desires to save the souls of the Mohammedans
and others, particularly such as are located in the immediate
vicinity of the sacred places," they will support Syria and try
and collapse Zionist efforts. Incidentally, Glazer writes, the
British had no choice but to calm down these "ultra-fanatics"
by slowing down Jewish immigration to Palestine. See "The
Proposed Constitution for Palestine," p. 19, where Glazer gives
a page discourse on France and partly on the Vatican.

231 "The Lodge of Palestine Resolution," p. 17.

232 Ibid.

233 However there were times that Lodge did call for American
intervention. For instance, he advised President McKinley
that he should intervene in Cuba, as the country, among
numerous characteristics listed, was in a "deplorable" state due
to the war and internal insurrection. He also notes that Cuba
is strategically important to the United States. For Lodge's
letter to the President, see *Record*, 54th Congress of the United

States., 1 Sess., Washington, DC, pp. 1971-72. There were also times, such as during the Cuban crisis of 1898, that Lodge called for war with Spain, and when he called for the American acquisition of the Philippines. He did support American involvement in World War I, yet often chastised the Wilson administration's handling of the conflict.

234 In a letter dated August 12, 1919, Senator Lodge implores and warns President Wilson not to join the League of Nations. Senate Archives, Washington DC, letter dated August 12, 1919, Lodge to Wilson. It should be noted that major general unrest among many Americans about US involvement abroad was widespread. Following World War I, America went through a transitional period known as "Red Scare", where, among other features, it manifested itself in American fear of entanglement in Europe. Fear of new values brought by European immigrants with communist and socialist backgrounds was also part of "Red Scare". This phobia, especially the former, played a significant role in the Republican takeover of Congress in 1918. See "The American Red Scare of 1919-1920," in R. Curry and T. Brown, *Conspiracy: The Fear of Subversion in American History* (New York: Holt, Rinehart and Winston, 1972), p. 145.

235 Combined Jewish Philanthropies, http://www.cjp.org/content_display.html?ArticleID=129998.

236 *The American Hebrew*, April 2, 1922, p. 666.

237 *The New Palestine*, April 28, 1922, p. 371.

238 On May 7, 1922, following the Senate adoption of a pro-Zionist resolution, *The New York Times* editorialized and questioned Lodge's motivation in supporting this resolution. "Is it in recognition of the League of Nation and under its mandate that Senator Lodge has pressed a resolution...or are there other mandates nearer his own home that have impelled the Senator from Massachusetts to this concern with the welfare of Palestine?" Quoted in *The New York Times*, May 1922, Section 2, p. 6.

239 The New Palestine, the official voice of the Zionist Organization of America, wrote that "The inspiration to have the American Government...express its favor of the establishment in Palestine of the Jewish National Home came from Senator Lodge himself...It was his own suggestion that it would be fitting and proper for the American Government officially to place itself on record in favor of the realization of the age-long hope of the Jewish people..." The New Palestine, March 31, 1922, p. 197.

240 For instance, as noted earlier Jewish "homeland" was
interpreted as 1) a British protectorate 2) an autonomous
Jewish region, yet "owned" by the British, and 3) a Jewish state.
Chaim Weizmann, the head of the World Zionist Organization,
used the phrase "Jewish commonwealth" to describe the
inference of the Balfour Declaration, setting off a storm among
British politicians, as it jumped to final status negotiations. It
should be noted that the first draft of the Declaration (July 1917)
stated that "His Majesty's Government accepts the principle
that Palestine should be reconstituted..." the key word here
being "that". Several months later, in August, a similar version
was drafted. However, the final version, released in November
1917, changed the wording to the following: "His Majesty's
Government view with favor the establishment *in* Palestine as a
national home..." the key word here being "in". The difference
of course is the eventual size of this Jewish national home. The
final draft was drawn up with the help of Edwin Montagu,
a Jew in the British Parliament who was a staunch opponent
of Zionism. Apparently, he was fearful of being accused of
having dual loyalties. This draft included League of Nations
ratification. See League of Nations, Mandate for Palestine,
Command #1785, Article 6, 1922.

241 All five of the following elements can be found in the SGP Box
269 2/3 entitled "The Proposed Constitution for Palestine,"
1920-1921, p. 21.

242 A distinction should be made between Jews from the "Old
Yishuv" and the "New *Yishuv*." The Old *Yishuv* was made up
of mainly religious Jews who moved to Palestine for religious
incentives. The New *Yishuv* was comprised of mainly secular
Jews who disdained much of the Orthodox lifestyle that the
Old *Yishuv* members practiced. Furthermore, the Old *Yishuv*,
in many ways, viewed the New *Yishuv* as a usurper of Jewish
values. For more on this, see Benjamin Ish-Shalom, *Rav
Avraham Itzhak HaCohen Kook: Between Rationalism and Mysticism*
(New York: State University of New York Press, 1993), pp. 11-15
and all notes.

243 It is indeed intriguing that so many American politicians
supported Zionism in the early 1920s, seeing that Zionism was
dominated by socialists, such as the Labor Party's David Ben-
Gurion, the dominant political figure in Palestine for years to
come. See, for instance, Walter Laqueur, *History of Zionism*
(New York: Schocken, 1989), p. 270. However, even though
many in the *Yishuv* had heavy socialist leanings, other powerful

Jews and Zionist groups opposed socialist dealings, such as Zev Jabotinsky, founder of Revisionist Zionist, and in America, Louis Brandeis. Both heavily favored the capitalist system, which may have helped convince numerous politicians that the Jews, if they set up a state, would be democratic capitalists.

244 Throughout the quest of obtaining support for Zionism, sentiments that Zionism resembled American values were widespread and often publicized. Some describes Zionist settlers in Palestine as "the Jewish Puritan", and numerous Jewish colonies as "the Jamestown and the Plymouth of the new House of Israel." The Jews were "building the new Judea even as the Puritans built a new England." Many of these sentiments were written by Bernard Rosenblatt, an American representative on the Palestine Zionist Executive. He wrote two articles in *The New York Times* in 1922 describing the positive and "American" spirit of the Zionists. Partially, comparing the Zionist to the American pioneers was in response to some who charged that Zionism was a socialist movement that mimicked Russia. For Rosenblatt's articles, see *The New York Times*, June 11, 1922, and June 25 1922.

245 The drafters of this document compare the Jews and Arabs potential grievances to those of French and British ancestry living in Quebec, Montreal.

246 Ibid. p. 21. The reason why the populations between Jew and Arab were so great was because Jewish migration was still in its early stages. By 1948, when Israel was created, the Jewish population of Palestine was some 650,000 while the Arab population was 1.2 million. See, Paul Mendes Flohr and Jehuda Reinharz, *The Jew in the Modern World*, p. 705.

247 Ibid. p. 22.

248 However, Lord Balfour, replying to the issue that 91% of Palestine was Arab, remarked that "Zionism...is...of far profounder import than the desires and prejudices of 700,000 Arabs who now inhabit that ancient land." From a letter from Weizmann to Lord Curzon, August 11, 1919, in Doreen Ingrams, *Palestine Papers 1917-1922: Seeds of Conflict* (George Braziller: NY), 197, p. 73.

249 For example the Sykes-Picot Agreement of 1916.

250 It should be noted that following the issuance of the Balfour Declaration, the Italian Government by the Italian ambassador to Great Britain said that:

On the instruction of His Excellency Baron Sonnino, His
Majesty's Minister for Foreign Affairs, I have the honor
to inform you that His Majesty's Government is pleased
to confirm the declaration already made through their
representatives in Washington. The Hague, and Salonica,
to the effect that they will use their best endeavors to
facilitate the establishment in Palestine of a Jewish national
center, it being understood that this shall not prejudice
the legal or political status enjoyed by Jews in any other
country.

Additionally according to the Zionist movement, the
French Government made the following announcement:

M. Sokolow, representing the Zionist organizations,
was received today by M. Stephen Pichon. M. Pichon
was happy to reaffirm that the understanding is complete
between the French and the British Governments
concerning the question of the Jewish establishment in
Palestine.

Additionally, Japan, Greece, Holland, Serbia, China,
and Siam, have likewise approved of the Balfour
Declaration. Congressmen during the Resolution debate
often invoked the approval of other world bodies for
the Balfour Declaration. See *Congressional Record House*
"National Home for the Jewish People" House Resolution
360 (Rept. NO. 1172), pp. 9815-9820.

251 On August 18, 1918, Wilson released a statement in favor of the
Balfour Declaration, though many claim that it fell short of a
full endorsement. For more on Wilson's partial endorsement of
the Balfour Declaration, see Arthur Walworth, *Wilson and His
Peacemakers: American Diplomacy at the Paris Peace Conference,
1919* (Norton & Co: New York & London, 1986), p. 479.

252 Wilson did not retract his statement. Arthur Walworth, *Wilson
and His Peacemakers: American Diplomacy at the Paris Peace
Conference, 1919* (New York & London: WW Norton & Co,
1986), p. 481.

253 Jastrow to Wilson, March 4, 1919. Arthur S. Link, ed., *The Papers
of Woodrow Wilson*, (Princeton: Princeton University Press,
1986), 55, pp. 438-39. This is the same Jastrow that produced
the popular Aramaic dictionary.

254 Henry King: President of Oberlin College in Ohio. He was
appointed to the Commission because of his close association

with anti-Zionist Protestant missionaries. Richard Crane was a philanthropist and one time close associate of Brandeis. However he became an anti-Zionist and Arab sympathizer.

255 From the Diary of Ray Stannard Baker, March 8. Ray Sannard Barker, *Woodrow Wilson and World Settlement* vol. II (Gloucester, MA: Doubleday, 1960 - originally published in 1922 -), vol. II, pp. 205- 219.

256 Ibid.

257 Wilson to Frankfurter, May 16, 1919. Cited from Link., ed. *The Papers of Woodrow Wilson*, vol. 59, p. 50.

258 The San Remo Conference and The British Mandate for Palestine, April 24, 1924. However, the document consisting of 28 Articles was ratified on July 24, 1920.

259 Elihu also participated in the defeat of Brandeis and the selection of Weizmann in the Zionist movement.

260 On March 22, 1922, one week prior to the Massachusetts Legislature's endorsement of a Jewish state, *The New Palestine*, the official voice of the Zionist Organization of America, wrote that "The inspiration to have the American Government... express its favor of the establishment in Palestine of the Jewish National Home came from Senator Lodge himself...It was his own suggestion that it would be fitting and proper for the American Government officially to place itself on record in favor of the realization of the age-long hope of the Jewish people..." *The New Palestine*, March 31, 1922, p. 197. See also Herbert Parzen, "The Lodge-Fish Resolution," in *American Jewish Historical Quarterly* (1970-1971), vol. 60, p. 4.

261 Proceedings of the Massachusetts General Court, March 29, 1922. The Massachusetts Resolution is printed in the *Congressional Record*, vol. 62, part 5, p. 4,758.

262 Information from *The New Palestine*, April 7, 1922, p. 222.

263 The information regarding the Speaker of the House escorting the Zionist delegation to Senator Lodge is known from a letter from Elihu Stone of Massachusetts, in a letter he sent to Zev Jabotinsky. Also, Stone notes that Lodge showed the Secretary of State the resolution on the subsequent day. The letters are dated April 15, 1922 and March 31, 1922, respectively and are found in the Zionist Archives and Library in New York City.

264 Quoted in Kosofsky, Scott Martin. *From Boston Jews and American Zionism*, Yale University Press, 2005, p. 263.

265 SGP Box 269 2/3 entitled "The Proposed Constitution for Palestine," 1920-1921, p. 22.

266 Ibid. pp. 22-23.

267 Ibid. p. 23.

268 Glazer and the ZOA also contacted Senator Charles Curtis. In a telegram dated December 12, 1921, Glazer implored Curtis to do all he could in assuring that the Senate would introduce and pass the Palestine resolution. SGP Box 269 1/5 "Charles Curtis" papers, entitled "Western Union Telegram," dated December 12, 1921 from Glazer to Curtis. In mid-January, Glazer's team returned to Washington and met with Curtis. The meeting was successful and Curtis, once again, committed himself to help the Jewish people to the best of his ability to create a Jewish home in Palestine. "Charles Curtis" papers, entitled "United States Senate, Committee on Rule," dated January 17, 1922 from Curtis to Glazer.

269 SGP Box 269 1/5 "Charles Curtis" papers, entitled "Western Union Telegram," dated December 12, 1921 from Glazer to Curtis.

270 Ibid. Entitled "United States Senate, Committee on Rules," dated December 14, 1921 from Curtis to Glazer.

271 Ibid. Letter dated December 26, 1921 from Curtis to Glazer.

272 "Charles Curtis" papers, entitled "United States Senate, Committee on Rule," dated January 17, 1922 from Curtis to Glazer.

273 Curtis was part Kaw Indian, and his mother was the granddaughter of Kansas-Kaw Chief, White Plume.

274 It should be noted that, as late as the 1890s, the American Israelite periodical claimed that Native American who either edited or ran Jewish owned newspapers were glaringly anti-Zionist. See *American Israelite*, January 13, 1898; October 19, 1899. See also Naomi Weiner Cohen, "The Reaction of Reform Judaism in America to Political Zionism (1897-1922)", in American Jewish Historical Society (Sep. 1950-June 1951, p. 369.

275 *The New York Times*, April 12, 1922, p. 3.

276 Resolution 191, 67th Congress, 2nd Session, *Congressional Record*, vol. 62 (LXII), part 5, p. 5376. Following the introduction at the Senate, the resolution was referred to the Committee on Foreign Relations. Note that the United States Resolution was more detailed than the Balfour Declaration, in particular when refereeing to "holy places and religious buildings." The Balfour Declaration does not state that religious sites be protected, and it has been surmised that the American version placed this line

in the resolution to pacify the Vatican and Christian groups in the United States. Also, Lodge calls for the establishment "of the National Home" in distinction from the Balfour Declaration that calls for the establishment of "a national home". See next chapter for more details.

277 *The New York Times*, April 5, 1922, p. 3. See also House Congressional Resolution 52, 67th Congress, 2nd Session. It was later asserted in 1953 by Louis Lipsky, head of the ZOA, that Fish brought this resolution to the House Floor because of the influence of Abraham Goldberg. Fish, it was claimed, stated the Judge Julian Mack and Rabbi Stephen Wise helped draft the wording of the resolution. It was also claimed that Fish brought this resolution to the House Floor for "humanitarian reasons". See Irwin Order, "American Zionism and the Congressional Resolution of 1922 on Palestine," in *American Jewish Historical Society*, p. 42 as well as note 1, where Order describes these events, apparently from both an interview with Louis Lipsky as well as from a letter from Fish to Order on June 26, 1953.

278 "Commends" was added in place of "support" at the suggestion of Secretary of State Hughes.

279 *Congressional Record*, 67th Congress, 2nd Session, House of Representative, April 4, 1922, p. 5035.

280 It was also noted that in the Lodge version, he calls for the establishment "of the National Home" in distinction from the Balfour Declaration, which calls for the establishment of "a national home".

281 Congressional Record House "National Home for the Jewish People" House Resolution 360 (Rept. NO. 1172), pp. 9801-9802.

282 From Herbert Parzen, "The Lodge-Fish Resolution" in American Jewish Historical Quarterly (Sep, 1970-June 1971), vol. 60, p. 75.

283 *Palestine*, vol. I, no. 3 (Feb. 1944), pp. 6-7.

284 New Palestine, vol. II, no. 17 (May 5, 1922), p. 280.

285 Congressional Record, vol. 62 (LXII), part 6, p. 6240.

286 If the Lodge Resolution was tied to the League of Nations mandate, it was feared that United States policy could be construed as supporting both the League's system and the settlement of the Near East, something many isolationists feared.

287 Cited from Order, *American Jewish Historical Society*, p. 44.

288 *The New York Times*, May 7, 1922, Section 2, p. 6. See also ibid.

289 See again *Congressional Record*, vol. LXII, part 6, p. 6240 and

Congressional Record House "National Home for the Jewish People" House Resolution 360 (Rept. NO. 1172), p. 9812.

290 *New Palestine*, vol. II, no. 17 (May 5, 1922), pp. 280-281.

291 Simon Glazer Box 269, letter from Goldberg to Glazer, March 3, 1922, American Jewish Archives. The letter highlights the need to fight anti-Semitism and anti-Zionism.

292 *The American Hebrew*, April 28, 1922, p. 222.

293 Parzen, "The Lodge-Fish Resolution," in *AJHQ*, p. 73.

294 Committee on Foreign Affairs, *Hearings*, pp. 1-2. See also ibid.

295 Ibid.

296 Congressional Record House "National Home for the Jewish People" House Resolution 360 (Rept. NO. 1172), p. 9804.

297 *Palestine*, vol. I, no 3 (Feb. 1944), p. 7.

298 Basically these resolutions were prepared by various Jewish organizations from the Congressmen's districts.

299 Committee on Foreign Affairs, *Hearings*, p. 1.

300 Frank Manuel, p. 169, claims that President Wilson did not necessarily approve the Balfour Declaration before it was announced; he merely "let it happen."

301 Establishment of a National Home in Palestine, Hearing before the Committee on Foreign Affairs, 67th Congress, 2nd Session on House Congressional Resolution 52 (Washington, D.C., 1922), p. 102.

302 Ibid. He said "I object to any country being called the national home of the Jewish people. America is my national home."

303 *The American Hebrew*, June 23, 1922, p. 152.

304 United States Congress, House of Representative, 67th Congress, 2nd Session, Hearing Before the Committee on Foreign Affairs on House Congressional Resolution 52 (Washington, DC, 1922), pp. 1, 65-67, 99-116. See also Cohen, "The Reaction of Reform Judaism in America to Political Zionism (189701922)," in *American Jewish Historical Society*, p. 391.

305 The Pittsburg Platform, in conjunction with the denial of Jewish nationhood, included the denying of the Davidic dynasty. The movement withdrew all references to the restoration of David and the return to the Land of Israel from their prayer books. See Central Conference of American Rabbis, *Yearbook*, vol. 1, pp. 80-125. For some of the developments of Reform ideology in regards to prayer and the omission of various themes such as the Davidic dynasty, see Lou H. Silberman,

"The Union Prayer Book: A Study in Liturgical Development,"
in *Retrospect and Prospect*, ed. Bertam Wallace Korn (New York:
Central Conference of American Rabbis, 1965), pp. 46-80; Jakob
J. Petuchowski, "From Censorship Prevention to Theological
Reform," in *HUCA* 50-51 (1969-70), pp. 299-324. The position
that Jews no longer constitute a nation was maintained for
many years after the Platform was accepted and radical
elements from the Platform could be found in all practical levels
of the Reform movement. On this, see Herbert Parzen, "The
Purge of the Dissidents: Hebrew Union College and Zionism,
1903-1907," in *Jewish Social Studies* 37 (Spring-Fall 1975), pp.
291-322. See also my "In the Plains of the Wilderness", pp. 81-
82.

306 In the Cleveland Conference of 1890 previous resolutions
stretching back years were considered for ratification.
Conference resolutions from the 1845 Frankfurt Conference,
as well as from 1869 at the Philadelphia Conference and in the
Pittsburg Conference in1885, were discussed. See again my, "In
the Plains of the Wilderness," pp. 81-82.

307 Central Conference of American Rabbis, *Yearbook*, vol. 7, pp. xli.

308 Central Conference of American Rabbis, *Yearbook*, vol. 16, pp.
180-183, and vol. 23, p. 108.

309 Ibid. vol. 28, pp. 133-134, vol. 30, pp. 140-141.

310 Union of American Hebrew Congregations, *Proceedings*, vol.
9, pp. 8520-8521. See also Cohen, "The Reaction of Reform
Judaism in America to Political Zionism (1897-1922)," in
American Jewish Historical Society, pp. 384-85.

311 Parzen cites *The New Palestine*, April 28, 1922, p. 253 where
Philipson remarks that "What right has the United States
Government to take sides in what is really an internal question
in an American religious communion?" It should be noted
that it would not be until 1937 that the Reform movement
officially retracted its anti-Zionist stance. Mike Meyer, *Response
to Modernity*, p. 319. One of the arguments that allowed for
this debate and the eventual ratification supporting Zionism
is found in the language of the Pittsburgh Platform, where it
states that Jews "no longer constituted a nation." However,
once Jews were becoming a nation, then they could support
the Zionist cause. On this, see Henry L. Feingold, *A Time for
Searching: Entering the Mainstream, 1920-1945* (Baltimore and
London: The John Hopkins University Press, 1992), p. 101. It
should be stated that even though most Reform leaders, as early

as the 1880s were anti-Zionist, some were not. See, for instance, Meyer, *Response to Modernity*, pp. 290-95.

312 See Allen C. Brownfeld's article Washington Report on Middle East Affairs, October-November 1999, pp. 83-84.

313 Congressman Chandler served New York's 19th District in Manhattan and was a longtime defender of Jews and Jewish rights worldwide, including for Palestine. He was a devout Christian. See references regarding Chandler's contributions to Jewish causes, and to many others as well: http://photos.state.gov/libraries/estonia/99874/History%20stories/Walter-M_-Chandler.pdf

314 Chandler is recorded as quoted Philipson in the debate. See Congressional Record House "National Home for the Jewish People" House Resolution 360 (Rept. NO. 1172), p. 9809-9820. Chandler stated the following " Mr. Speaker, I respectfully submit that the attitude of Doctor Philipson and of the Jews of the Union of American Hebrew Congregations at Richmond and their attempt to define Jewish citizenship and nationality are nothing new in history. They are merely a revival of recurring inquiries and discussions of the subject that have taken place in every age of the world since the beginning of the Jewish dispersion. I ask the indulgence of the House while I discuss briefly this phase of the subject." Chandler then goes into a lengthy discourse of Jewish history from the destruction of the Second Temple through Napoleon's Sanhedrin and more.

315 Simon Glazer Box, American Jewish Archives, "Charles Curtis" papers, entitled "Western Union Telegram," dated April 18, 1922 from Glazer to Curtis. Glazer also wrote in the letter that President Harding, while he met with Glazer on November 18, 1921, fully agreed that a resolution was necessary and that he later spoke with Arthur Balfour about the matter.

316 "Charles Curtis" papers, entitled "United States Senate, Committee on Rules," dated April 10, 1922 from Curtis to Glazer. There appears from Glazer's writing that one other group opposed the resolution, namely an "ultra-radical" wing of American Jewry led by Morgenthau. Louis Lipsky, the General Secretary of the ZOA wired Glazer and told him that he would contact Senator Lodge and urge him to make haste. "Charles Curtis" papers, entitled "Western Union Telegram," dated April 24, 1922.

317 Some of the next paragraph is taken from Parzen, *American Jewish Historical Quarterly*, p. 77.

318 *The New Palestine*, April 28, 1922, p. 263.

319 This despite Turkish inhibitions. See Parzen, *American Jewish Historical Quarterly*, p. 77.

320 Information from the David S. Wyman Institute for Holocaust Studies, October 23, 2005. http://www.wymaninstitute.org/press/2005-10-23.php. Concocted by the Tsarist disinformation service around 1895, the *Protocols* has served for more than a century as a worldwide propaganda tool against the Jews. The forgery presents a detailed account of a Jewish plot to take over the world, both economically and politically. (The *Protocols* are even invoked today by various militia groups in America, Russia, and Japan as well as extensively throughout the Middle East). The publication, however, is in no way a serious scholarly work. The *Protocols* have had an enormous impact over the years and it has been described, almost accurately, as "a warrant for genocide." See my work, "In the Plains of the Wilderness", pp. 136-137, as well as Norman Cohn, *Warrant for Genocide: The Myth of the Jewish World-Conspiracy and the Protocols of the Elders of Zion* (London, 1967).

321 Aside from labeling Zionism as "Bolsheviski" Shatara likened the Zionist project to that of socialism, which irked the tongue of Congressman Henry Allen Cooper of Wisconsin, who said "do you think the Jew ...proverbially a believer in private property, would circulate any law that would destroy private property?" Hearings Before the Committee on Foreign Relations, House of Representatives, House Continuing Resolution No. 52, April 19-21, 1922, p. 156.

322 On April 11, 1921 riots broke out in Jaffa, leaving around 45 Jews and 48 Arab dead. The Zionists maintained that the riots were instigated by Haj Amin el-Husseini, the Grand Mufti of Jerusalem, a bitter opponent of Zionism and the Jews, while the Arabs maintained that the riots started when two rival Jewish groups, one supporting Bolshevism, the other Socialism, starting brawling in Jaffa. The Arabs subsequently heard fighting and believed they were under attack and started fighting the Jews. Totah and Shakara no doubt believed the latter account. Subsequent to the outburst of riots during 1920-1921, the Haycraft Commission that Britain assigned to investigate the happenings warned that Jewish immigration was the main catalyst behind Arab discomfort. Hence, the Jews were blamed for the riots. See my "In the Plains of the Wilderness", pp. 121-22.

323 See Order, *American Jewish Historical Society*, p. 45.

324 Ibid. p. 46.

325 For both ideas, see Ibid.

326 *Congressional Record*, House of Representative, April 18, 1922, p. 5,693.

327 Parzen, *American Jewish Historical Quarterly*, p. 78.

328 *Congressional Record*, House of Representative, May 3, 1922, p. 6,289.

329 Parzen, *American Jewish Historical Quarterly*, p. 79. Parzen notes that the removal of any Diaspora references was originally a request from British anti-Zionists to those formulating the Balfour Declaration in England. The Zionists were pleased with its erasure. He cites *Congressional Record*, Senate, May 3, 1922, p. 6,240.

330 Simon Glazer Box 269, American Jewish Archives, folder entitled "The Palestine Lodge Resolution," p. 1.

331 House Joint Resolution 322, *Congressional Record*, vol. 62, part 10, p. 9,799; *The New Palestine*, vol. 2, no 20 (May 26, 1922, p. 330). Also, see Parzen, p. 79.

332 House of Representatives 1038, 67th Congress, 2nd Session, May 31, 1922. Also cited in Order, *American Jewish Historical Society*, pp. 46-47.

333 *The New York Times*, May 28, 1922, Section 2, p. 4; Order, *American Jewish Historical Society*, p. 47.

334 *Congressional Record*, vol. 62, part 10, p. 9,799.

335 *Congressional Record*, House of Representatives, June 30, 1922, p. 10,549.

336 The more popular studies, which spans generations, are Melvin Urofsky, *American Zionism from Herzl to the Holocaust* (Lincoln: University of Nebraska Press, 1975); Philip J. Baram, *The Department of State in the Middle East 1919-1945* (Philadelphia: University of Pennsylvania Press, 1978); Frank E. Manuel, *The Realities of American-Palestine Relations* (Washington, D.C.: Public Affairs Press, 1949); John DeNovo, *American Interests and Policies in the Middle East*, 1900-1939 (Minneapolis: University of Minnesota Press, 1963.

337 It was said that Lansing stated his disappointment "bitterly". See Joan Eisner. *American Policy Towards Palestine 1916-1948*. M.A. Thesis, New York University 1955, pp. 4-5.

338 Frank E. Manuel. *The Realities of American-Palestine Relations*,

Washington, DC: Public Affairs Press, 1949, p. 172, where Lansing is said to have told Wilson "to go slowly" on the Zionist question. Philip J. Baram, the next generation of scholars that studied the State Department, also believed that the less the United States had to do with Zionism the better. See Baram, *The Department of State in the Middle East 1919-1945* (Philadelphia: University of Pennsylvania Press, 1978), p. 53. 12 Ibid., p. 262.

339 In contradistinction to Lansing and others that asserted the Jews themselves were not united on the Zionist cause, the view in the House of Representatives during the Lodge-Fish Resolution's debate could not have been more divergent. It was important for Congress to factually know and believe that the Jews were united in this cause. Many a congressman openly stated that vast majority American Jewry supported a government endorsement of the Balfour Declaration and Zionism. Congressman Walter M. Chandler of New York, in a rather lengthy speech to the Congress in support of the Resolution stated that:

"Another cogent political reason is that an overwhelming majority of the approximately 3,000,000 Jews of America desire the passage of this resolution and we should certainly pay some little respect to the desires of so important and respectable an element of our population and citizenship, especially when the action contemplated can do no possible harm to the balance of the country.

But how do you know, you may ask, that the majority of American Jews desire the passage of this resolution? I candidly admit that there has been no direct referendum on the subject among the Jews themselves, but I learned from the hearings before the Foreign Affairs Committee that there was an American Jewish Congress held not very long ago at Philadelphia at which delegates representing some 360,000 Jewish voters adopted a resolution by a practically unanimous vote indorsing the Zionist movement. In this connection I wish to quote a paragraph from the hearings containing the statement of Mr. Louis Lipsky, of New York City, who represented the Zionist Organization of America:

The Jews of the United States held a congress two years ago after the Balfour Declaration of the British

Government, prior to the peace conference. There were over 360,000 Jews who voted for the delegates who attended that congress. In addition to the 360,000 voters, who elected 200 delegates, there were also 100 delegates elected by the following organizations, practically every national Jewish organization: The American Jewish Committee, of which Mr. Luis Marshall is chairman; the Independent Order B'nai B'rith, of which Mr. Adolph Kraus, of Chicago, is chairman; the Order B'rith Abraham; the Association of Orthodox Rabbis; the Independent Western Star Order; the Independent Workmen's Circle of America; the Progressive Order of the West; the United Synagogues of America, composed of the conservative congregations in the United States; the United Hebrew Trades, which represents an association of the Jewish trade-unions in New York City; the faculty of the Rabbinical College of America, of which Dr. Ryell is the President; the Union of Orthodox Jewish Congregations, which is an organization of Orthodox Jewish congregations somewhat similar to the United Synagogues, except that it is more orthodox. The United Synagogues of America represents those organizations that are affiliated with the Jewish Theological Seminary in New York, of which the late Doctor Schechter was president.

At this congress the following resolutions were adopted practically unanimously. There was one gentleman who voted against them. It seems to me that the endorsement of the Zionist movement by an American Jewish congress, composed of delegates who were elected by the votes of 360,000 American Jews, is very good proof that the Jews of America very generally favor the pending resolution.

Additionally, to note one other figure, Congressman Albert Rossdale of New York, who said that:

It has been said that there were objections to a Jewish Palestine by some of the Jewish people themselves. To be sure there are some Jews who are indifferent, but that is because they have largely drifted away from their own people or know little or nothing about the movement. These protesting Jewish anti-Zionists constitute barely one-half of one percent of the race. The great majority of the Jewish people in the United States and elsewhere are enthusiastic supporters and advocates of Zionism... See *Congressional Record House* "National Home for the Jewish People" House Resolution 360 (Rept. NO. 1172), pp. 9799-9820 for many similar quotes by members of the House.

340 *FRUS 1920 = Papers Relating to the Foreign Relations of the United States 1920.* Washington, DC, p. 2:71.

341 Frank E. Manuel. *The Realities of American-Palestine Relations,* Washington, DC: Public Affairs Press, 1949, p. 167. Lansing attempted to use his influence to persuade Wilson not to endorse the Balfour Declaration. See Manuel, p. 216.

342 Edward Meade Earle, "Oil and American Foreign Policy" in *New Republic* 20 Aug. 1924, pp. 355-357.

343 Frank E. Manuel. *The Realities of American-Palestine Relations.* Washington, DC: Public Affairs Press, 1949, p. 271. Not to digress too far from the chapter at hand, oil, however, may have been a factor, although certainly not a primary one, in both England and the United States' policy decisions regarding to Zionism. Elements throughout both governments, particularly, as noted, in the President's/Prime Minister's Cabinet, and those who work for him, i.e. the State Department and Foreign Ministry, often worked against each other. As for the United States and its oil program, the American-Palestine Company was established in Palestine in 1921 in order to begin the search and ultimate development of oil there. See Bernard DeNovo, *American Interests and Policies in the Middle East 1900-1939* (Minneapolis: University Press of Minnesota, 1963), p. 339.

344 American Jewish Historical Quarterly, March, 1974, p. 47

345 Bernard DeNovo, *American Interests and Policies in the Middle East 1900-*1939, p, 340, 344.

346 *Records of the Department of State* 867n.01/1287, p. 12. Internal Near East Desk memo dated 4/1/38. Some believe that Hughes wasn't per say against the resolution, and proof that is cited for this idea is that he actually met with Lodge and went over the document. This, however, is highly speculative. Lodge had the power to bring Hughes in to state his views, not the other way around.

347 Urofsky, *American Zionism from Herzl to the Holocaust,* ibid., pp. 307-308.

348 Evans, Laurence, *United States Policy and the Partition of Turkey 1914-1924.* Baltimore: Johns Hopkins University Press, 1965, p. 265.

349 Frank E. Manuel. *The Realities of American-Palestine Relations.* Washington, DC: Public Affairs Press, 1949, p. 278.

350 Chaim Weizmann, *Trial and Error* (N.Y.: Harper, 1949), pp. 431-432. For more on Zionism's leaders, especially Stephen Wise's sentiments regarding the State Department (Wise was an active leader of Zionism), see Carl Hemann Voss, ed., *Stephen S. Wise, Servant of The People: Selected Letters* (Philadelphia: Jewish Publication Society, 1970), p. 252. See also Melvin Urofsky, *American Zionism from Herzl to the Holocaust*, p. 408. Frank E. Manuel, *The Realities of American-Palestine Relations* also lambastes the Department of State for its treatment of Zionism, especially in its infant years following the Balfour Declaration. See Manuel p. 305.

351 Lawrence Davidson, in an essay in the Middle East Policy Council, asserts that Manuel, Baram and others are incorrect in their assumption regarding State Department sentiments. He claims they didn't analyze the American economic involvement in the region, which he asserts, is a main reason why the State Department opposed Zionism. Meaning, it was not just because of anti-Jewish sentiment or for the potential antagonizing of Turkey (only during World War I), but American financial interests. See Davidson, *The State Department and Zionism, 1917-1945, A Reevaluation*, Vol. 7, Oct. 1999, #1, pp. 21-37. Davidson also surmises that the reason for Hughes' opposition to Zionism may have also stemmed from the fact that a peace treaty with Turkey, post World War I, had not been secured, and therefore the legal status of Palestine, and American rights there had yet to be determined. Hughes, Davidson argues, may not have wanted to upset the balance of power until American interests were secured, which he believed would be in danger by the United States supporting Zionism. However, it is unlikely that this sort of "revisionist" thinking, though interesting, is accurate. See Davidson pp. 25-26.

352 Manual asserts that Dulles was trying to wreck the Balfour Declaration. See Manuel. *The Realities of American-Palestine Relations* pp. 277-279.

353 *Records of the Department of State*, 867n.01/227, Dulles to Harrison, dated 5/26/22. Cited in Davidson, p. 28.

354 *Records of the Department of State*, 867n.01/227, Dulles to Harrison, dated 5/26/22.

355 *New Palestine*, vol. 2, no. 17, May 5, 1922, pp. 280-281.

356 The preamble (both for the Senate and House), it should be

recalled, states that "Whereas owing to the outcome of many centuries the Jewish people believed in and yearned for the rebuilding of their ancient homeland: and whereas, owing to the outcome of the World War and their part therein, the Jewish people are to be enabled to recreate....

357 *Congressional Record*, Senate, July 12, 1922, p. 10,210.

358 *Congressional Record*, House of Representatives, September 11, 1922, p. 12,368.

359 Letter from the State Department to George Christina, President Harding's secretary, in the National Archives, State Department File 867 N. 01/311A. Cited in Order, p. 47.

360 Note that the Lodge-Fish Resolution is more detailed than the Balfour Declaration, specifically in regards to the protection of holy places and religious buildings, which is not mentioned in the Balfour Declaration. This last line was inserted to placate the Vatican.

361 On June 25, 1922, more than a month after the Senate passed its pro-Zionist resolution, but prior to the House passing theirs, President Harding wrote to the Zionist Organization of America, at its twenty-fifth annual convention in Philadelphia. He said that "A long time interest, both sentimental and practical, in the Zionist movement cause me to wish that I might meet the members of the organization and express the esteem which I feel in behalf of the great movement." Later, Harding remarked that: "I am very glad to express my approval and hearty sympathy for the effort of the Palestine foundation fund in behalf of the restoration of Palestine as a homeland for the Jewish people. I have always viewed with an interest which, I think is quite as much practical as sentimental the proposal for the rehabilitation of Palestine, and I hope the effort now being carried on in this and other countries in this behalf may meet with the fullest measure of success." See *Congressional Record House* "National Home for the Jewish People" House Resolution 360 (Rept. NO. 1172), pp. 9814-9815.

362 Ibid. pp. 281-82.

363 In fact, Brandeis once remarked that "Let no American imagine that Zionism is incompatible with patriotism. Multiple loyalties are objectionable only if they are inconsistent." See Louis D. Brandeis, "The Jewish Problem: How to solve It," *Brandeis on Zionism: A Collection of Addresses and Statements*, forwarded by Felix Frankfurter, ed. Solomon Goldman (Washington D.C.: The Zionist Organization of America, 1942).

364 Most notably praise came from the ZOA. Abraham Goldberg, who sat on the Administrative Committee, wrote Glazer as early as May 4 to congratulate and extend his organizations recognition and appreciation to him. Goldberg said that "It would be a crime if I would forget you at the time of our joy" and that "the credit should be accorded to the one to whom it is due." See "Administrative Committee, Zionist Organization of America," letter dated May 4, 1922 from Goldberg to Glazer. In a telegram on the same day, Louis Lipsky congratulated Glazer for his success with the Senate. See Ibid. entitled "Western Union Telegram," dated May 4, 1922 from Lipsky to Glazer.

365 See, for instance, all letters from the "United States Senate, Committee on Rules" dated after May 3, 1921. Several letters from the "Administrative Committee, Zionist Organization of America," also dated after May 3, praise Glazer. In numerous letters, Senator Curtis stated that "it was a pleasure to assist you in the resolution and I am glad favorable action was had in the Senate." See "Charles Curtis" papers, letter dated May 11, 1922 and June 13, 1922. See also the letter entitled "Weinfeild, Sperber and Levine," lawyers and friends of Glazer from his days in Montreal where they state that the proper public recognition for Glazer has not yet reached its peak. The letter is dated November 3, 1922 from Marcus M. Sperber to Glazer (this letter, as opposed to some of the previous ones just mentioned, came after the President signed the joint resolution).

366 A good portion of the pamphlet was utilized for this book. Glazer sent Senator Curtis a copy in early October 1922. See Ibid. Letter dated October 3, 1922.

367 By August 1923, Glazer was on a crusade to convince the two New York Senators to support the cause. See ibid. Letter dated August 2, 1923 from Curtis to Glazer. Curtis, on the request of Glazer, wrote a letter of recommendation for Glazer to speak to the Senators.

368 See "Administrative Committee, Zionist Organization of America 1/17 folder entitled "Palestine Immigration," letter dated October 24, 1923 from Curtis to the Secretary of the President C.B. Slemp.

369 Ibid. Letter dated October 26, 1923 from Glazer to Coolidge.

370 Ibid.

371 Ibid.

372 Ibid. Letter dated October 28, 1923 from Glazer to the Zionist Organization of America.

373 It was implied in the letter that Coolidge would eventually
speak with State as well. See the letter dated October 29, 1923
from Curtis to Glazer. See Also "Charles Curtis" papers, letter
dated October 29, 1923 from Curtis to Glazer. In a letter dated
November 5, 1923, C.B. Slemp, the Secretary to the President
also said that he personally had brought it up with the State
Department. See "Palestine Immigration," letter dated
November 5, 1923 from Slemp to Glazer.

374 This can be deduced from letters Glazer received from
Coolidge and Curtis, where both speak of the State Department
"reviewing" the matter. Apparently, State "reviewed" the
matter over a long period of time. See letters dated November
5 and 14, 1923 from Slemp to Glazer, and November 16 and 24,
1923 from Curtis to Glazer.

375 Ibid. Letter dated November 22, 1923 from Glazer to Slemp.

376 Ibid. Letter dated November 24, 1923 from Slemp to Glazer.

377 Ibid. Letter dated December 12, 1923 from Glazer to Slemp.
Glazer also wrote that President Harding knew of this.

378 Ibid.

379 "Charles Curtis" papers, letter dated March 7, 1928, from Glazer
to Curtis. Some Jews in New York had started the "Curtis
for President Club" hoping to make him a serious contender.
In any event, Curtis was selected as Herbert Hoover's Vice
President in 1928 and served that position until 1933.

380 Ibid. Letter dated March 7, 1928 from Glazer to Curtis.

381 Ibid. Letter dated March 29, 1928 from Glazer to Marvin.

382 Ibid. Letter dated March 31, 1932 from Glazer to Curtis. A
memorandum was sent to Curtis to approve of the proposal.
The land was to be bought in May of the same year and one
of the members of the rabbinical organization would go to
Palestine and purchase the land.

383 Ibid. Letter dated February 12, 1932 from Curtis to Glazer.
Curtis wanted to speak about this matter with Glazer when he
came to Washington, but said he had no objections if the Jews
wanted to name a town after him.

384 Ibid. Letter dated April 1, 1932 from Curtis to Glazer.

385 Manuel, Frank E., *The Realities of American-Palestine Relations*
(Washington DC: Public Affairs Press, 1949), p. 282 asserts
that Brandeis was a pivotal player in the passing of the joint
resolution.

386 The Palestine Lodge-Fish Resolution was invoked in the 1930s by President Roosevelt and later by Senators and Congressmen. For instance, on January 27, 1944, Congressman James A. Wright of Pennsylvania and Congressman Ranult Compton of Connecticut brought forth a resolution in the House of Representatives urging the White House and Congress to compel Great Britain to open Jewish immigration to Palestine without restriction with the intent that Palestine would become a Jewish commonwealth. A few days later, on February 1, 1944 Senator Robert Wagner of New York and Robert Taft of Ohio brought forth an identical resolution which was submitted to the Committee on Foreign Relations. The resolutions were brought forth in order to abolish the White Paper of 1939 which limited Jewish immigration to Palestine to 75,000 through 1945. Senator Wagner stated that the Lodge resolution confirmed the Balfour Declaration. Wagner said that "Although it was issued in the name of the British Government it was a matter of fact a joint policy of the Governments of Great Britain and the United States." See *The Canadian Jewish Review*, Vol. XXVI, front page column, Montreal, February 11, 1944.

387 "The Lodge of Palestine Resolution," p. 11.

Also By Paul Azous

In the Plains of the Wilderness:
Anthologies of Modern Jewish History
(Mazo Publishers, September 2006)

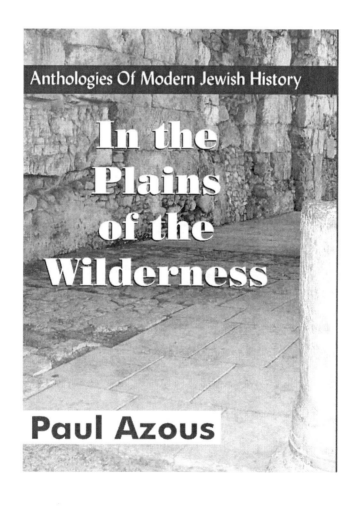

Lightning Source UK Ltd.
Milton Keynes UK
UKOW04f2242290713

214580UK00006B/844/P